GRANDMAMA'S
Treasured Favorites & Traditional Recipes

Many treasured moments in my kitchen, will always be wonderful memories, cooking or baking with my children, then with my grandchildren.

ISBN-13: 978-1492975779
ISBN-10: 149297577X
Copyright 2013 - Dianne Ireland

E-mail: dfireso1@telus.net

Cover Design and Art Work by – Dianne Ireland

Printed by Create Space

Disclaimer:
Many of these recipes are from before the 1930's and have come from many different old cook books, as well as from my childhood collection of recipes, family, relatives and friends shared recipes, which I have greatly enjoyed cooking or baking with.

I have experienced each and every one of these recipes and many of them countless times, as they became family favorites.

My favorite recipe book, and the one I have used often, is the "Ladies Auxiliary to the Royal Canadian Legion" which is showing its age, with tattered pages. This book was given to me by my mom for the 1987 Christmas.

Mom was notorious for writing dates on items she received or gifted.

Please read the directions of each recipe carefully before making. Cannot be responsible for any hazards, loss or damage that may occur as a result of any recipe used.

History of the Family Farm Kitchen Cupboard

Mom and Dad's farm kitchen cupboard was built by Mr. Joe Rabchak of Grimshaw, Alberta during the 1930's. The cupboard was constructed with various pieces of salvaged wood and wooden apple boxes for the two drawers. My dad, Steve Wurst traded a cow for the cupboard in the late 1940's. This old farm kitchen cupboard has seen many coats of paint, and is now in my home.

Dedicating this book to my loving family
Jim
Stephen & Chris
Jamie-Anne
Emily
Matthew
In memory Robert

Acknowledgements

Mom & Dad for their wisdom and teachings
To my five sisters and two brothers

Thank you to, two special ladies, Judy Coates &
Bernadette Harris, for taking the time to edit my book,
and their positive comments.

Wood Cook Stove

Farm Kitchen Cupboard

Preamble

"Looking Through Life's Teachings", from mother earth's garden of richness to the heart of our country farm kitchen to the current kitchen of today.

My inspiration for this book is to share memories; experiences and a collection of traditional and treasured favorite recipes, which played a big part in our family's everyday lives, special occasion's and family gatherings. Small, but special pieces of times gone by to share with family and friends.

Many young people raised in farming communities worked alongside their parents, helping with various chores outdoors and indoors. Being the oldest of my sisters and brothers, certain responsibilities became natural, helping with the planting, weeding and harvesting the vegetable garden, wild berry picking and general household chores, besides keeping an eye on the younger children. As the oldest in the family this was normal.

The outside farm chores were the responsibilities of my brothers. One thing I did want to do was drive the tractor, but, as I recall, my dad felt this was part of the boy's duties, and not for girls. Although mom often spent her spring and fall days out on the tractor cultivating the fields, while dad was in town working and we were at school.

At about 11 or 12 years of age, I started to learn to cook and bake on the polished black wood cook stove, which had a round stove pipe going up the back, along the wall, and through the ceiling to the chimney. On one side of the stove was a reservoir for water, which kept water warm from the heat of the stove, and on the opposite side were two round openings with covers. The wood was put into these holes where a fire would burn to heat the stove for cooking and baking, as well as keeping the house warm.

I remember the oven had multi uses, besides baking. When mittens or socks needed to be dried, mom would open the oven door and lay out the mitts and/or socks across the door. The heat from inside the oven would be enough for the drying process. At times, when it was colder than usual in the house, especially in the winter time, we would open the oven door, line up kitchen chairs in front of the open door and place our feet up onto the door to warm them. Can anyone imagine this picture today?

Kids in the garden

My baby sister

Each of us girls learned how to bake and cook under mom's watchful eye and steady direction. The stove needed to be kept filled with wood to ensure proper heat for both cooking and baking. I believe this was a skill in its self, and we soon learned this technique as quickly as we did other skills.

There were a number of experiments of various recipes served to my family members. Most of the comments were encouraging, but not all. At any one time around the farm kitchen table there were no less than ten people, tasting a new recipe or a revised one.

Eventually learning how to prepare meals using whatever was in the cupboard became natural, and by following a recipe became even more successful. A well learned lesson in itself.

Looking back, who would have thought that what we ate as youngsters on the farm, would actually show up on restaurant menu's decades later.

One of my many memories (or maybe a nightmare, when thinking of all those weeds) of growing up on the farm was the huge vegetable garden. This supplied the family with a variety of main dishes throughout the summer and into the fall, and then jars and jars of canned goods for the winter time. Just like clockwork, on the May long weekend, planting season began and we helped mom plant rows and rows of peas, carrots, beans, corn, potatoes, and a number of other vegetables, hoping the appropriate amount of rain would fall during the growing season.

As kids, we played hide n seek in the garden. We weren't supposed to, and hoped we didn't get caught. We were kids having great fun, hiding among the rows of corn, which grew tall. They were like small sapling trees with long straight green leaves and often grew to a height of five feet tall or more. Hey, what else was there to do when the chores where done?

I remember in the fall, harvest time, the huge piles of dug-up potatoes, drying in the warm sun before being sacked and placed in the cellar. The cellar was an 8' x 8' x 5' deep hole dug under the house. Dad had built wood framed shelves along one side for mom's canning jars and a crated area served as a potato bin. Those were the years when Mother Nature supplied us with plenty of food.

Kids on the tractor

In later years, gardening and growing flowers became natural, and I always have felt that need to plant something. Smelling the rich moist earth, digging and planting, gave me a sense of achievement. Spring arrives and it's time to plant seeds, and then nurture those tiny seeds of many colors and shapes to maturity. Just like a farmer, I moved from the farm, but you could never take the farm out of the kid.

At our homes in Brownvale and Grimshaw, I never seemed to have a large enough garden space, to grow the many varieties of plants as I would have liked.

So, when I moved with my husband and our three children, to our undeveloped acreage, I took advantage of this opportunity to have a large garden, to plant vegetables, fruit trees and herbs.

Breaking land for a garden would be new and exciting. My vision was a large garden, maybe not quite as large as the one on my childhood family farm, but BIG.

Staking out the chosen area was the first step. Our dear neighbor came with a tractor and plow to turn the earth into a rich soft moist soil for my garden plot.

When I first told him the size, he looked at me and said "are you sure?" I was thinking that he didn't think it was a good idea; however he did break the ground for me. What a garden I had! A variety of fresh vegetables, and lots and lots of canning, freezing and sacking of potatoes.

Every spring, as a family ritual, we planted the garden together. My husband Jim cultivated the soil to make it ready for planting, and the children helped with the planting of a variety of seeds.

Then, working together, we dug and dropped a seed potato into each hole and then covered the potato seed with our feet. Up and down each row we marched.

The garden grew, and of course so did the weeds and when it came time to weed, there were not many volunteers. Everyone had something more important to do. However, with some persuasion, the weeding of the garden was done, and then we would go to town, to spend time with friends and family.

Recipe of a Happy Day!!

1 cup friendly words
4 tsp. time and patience
Heaping dash of humor
2 cups understanding
Large pinch of warm personality

Measurer words carefully, add heaping cups of understanding. Stir, using generous amounts of time and patience. Keep temperatures low, do not boil. Add a dash of humor and a pinch of warm personality often. Season to taste with the spice of life. Serve in individual molds to all your friends and family.

Unknown Author

Much of the fresh produce coming from the garden was cooked or baked from my collection of treasured well-kept recipes

As a youngster, I started collecting interesting recipes, from newspapers and magazines. I took great care in cutting them out, with the intention of trying each recipe one day.

I couldn't imagine that, as a young girl collecting and saving all those pieces of papers and notes that I actually took time to type some out. Yes, typing on an old fashion non-electric type writer. We couldn't make corrections using spell check or cut and paste, as we do on our computers of today

What inspires someone to collect recipes? Going through all of my collection, I see some have notes on them; others have a name at the bottom of the recipe with well wishes, all of which brings back many memories.

Looking through my faded, yellowed, partial rips and torn corners of these sheets with a bit of musky smell I see a collection started by a young girl, interested in baking and cooking. I chuckle to myself, as I look at some of the recipes and wonder why? Then as I flip through the pages, I remember particular ones I used, and still use continuously and have become favorites. These are ones with hand written notes on -- REALLY GOOD or MAKES 3 DOZEN, or stained with dried food on the page.

We are talking fifty plus years ago, and I have carted my precious pieces of papers with me on every move I made, from getting married to each of our homes.

Searching through this collection going back fifty years, reminds me why I wish to incorporate all these favorites together. This is for those who enjoy trying new recipes, and for my family and friends to read the many stories that go along with many of these recipes, and cherish them for a very long time.

My treasured memories are of the nurturing of my garden, spending time in the kitchen with my children and then with my grandchildren and preparing special meals for my family and friends.

CONTENTS

Dianne, in the garden and sitting on the tractor.

Daughter, Jamie-Anne in the garden.

BREADS – BUNS

Bread

4 cups hot water
8 tbsps. sugar
4 tbsps. salt
4 tbsps. shortening
4 cups cold water
4 yeast pkgs. or 5 tbsps.
8 tbsps. lukewarm water
24 cups flour

Mix hot water, sugar and salt together, stir until dissolved. Add cold water and yeast; let it stand for about 5 minutes. Add lukewarm water and stir gently. Add 2 to 4 cups of flour at a time and mix until all 24 cups are mixed in. Knead the dough making sure all the flour is well mixed into soft dough. Pour warm shortening over top of dough, work shortening into dough. Continue to knead until the dough is an elastic texture. Let rise, punch down and let rise again. Once the dough has risen twice the dough is ready to make bread and/or buns. Prepare oven at 350 degrees F. Bake bread for 60 minutes and buns for 25 minutes until golden brown on top.

****

This bread recipe is approximately 100 years old and from the late Mrs. Margaret Greff, who lived in the Griffin Creek area near Berwyn, Alberta. I call this recipe a No Fail Bread recipe, because no matter where you live, or the varied warm temperatures of a room, the bread will rise and make perfect bread and/or buns.

Dough Goughs

Whatever these were supposed to be called, or maybe there is no name, but my mom called them dough gouges. What are they? Well, it is raw bread dough flattened, cut into whatever shape you desired, and deep fried. Once puffed and golden brown on one side then they are flipped to the other side to turn golden brown. Remove from oil and cool. When cooled, dip each piece into icing sugar. BEST EVER.

See Bread recipe-

****

These were treats when mom made them for us, and we certainly enjoyed them.

Cinnamon Buns

See Bread recipe-

Cinnamon Bun Mixture –
1 cup brown sugar
2 tbsps. margarine
3 tbsps. cinnamon
½ cup raisins – option
½ cup nuts - option

Take dough and roll out on a floured board or table, with a rolling pin until the dough is about 2 to 2 ½ inches thick. Spread margarine over the dough, and then sprinkle with brown sugar and cinnamon. Add raisins and nuts if desired. Starting with the dough edge on one side and roll until the dough is shaped in a long roll. Slice about 2 inches thick and place on a greased baking sheet. Let rise. Heat oven 350 degrees F and bake about 10 to 15 minutes.

Cinnamon Twist Knots

Cinnamon Twist Knot Mixture-
2 cups brown sugar
3 tbsps. cinnamon

Mix together in a bowl. Set aside.

½ cup oil
Warm in a pan until lukewarm.

Cut dough in 2" x 1" pieces, then stretch to a string like shape, dip into the pan of warm oil and then into the bowl of sugar mix until well coated. Twist dough into a knot and place on a greased baking sheet. Let rise. Heat oven 350 degrees F and bake about 10 to 12 minutes. Watch closely to make sure not to burn.

****

Making cinnamon buns with my children and now with my grandchildren always brings joy to my kitchen. No matter how many different sizes or shapes these buns have, a lot of love is put into them. After they are baked, and no matter what they looked like, they all taste delicious. I think the cinnamon twist knots are the favorites.

2 Hour Buns

3 cups lukewarm water
8 tbsps. sugar
6 tsps. oil
1 tsp. salt
2 tbsps. yeast- fast rising
2 eggs
7 – 8 cups flour or enough to make workable dough

In a large bowl beat eggs one at a time, add sugar, salt, oil and water, whip until well mixed. Add yeast, sugar and beat. Add flour until soft dough forms and knead until not sticky. Let rise for 15 minutes, punch down and let rise again for 15 minutes, ready to make buns. Let rise, then bake at 350 degrees F for about 25 minutes or until golden brown.

Sweet Roll

½ cup lukewarm water
2 tsps. sugar
2 yeast pkgs.
1 ½ cups lukewarm milk
½ cup sugar
2 tsps. salt
2 eggs
½ cup butter or margarine
6 ½ cups flour

Measure water into mixing bowl, add 2 tsps. sugar and stir until sugar is dissolved. Sprinkle yeast over water, let dissolve. Add milk, ½ cup sugar, salt, eggs, butter or margarine and half of flour. Beat until smooth. Add remainder of flour and mix until soft dough is formed. Make sure all flour is well mixed in. Knead, cover with cloth and let rise for 1 ½ hours. Roll dough into small round buns and place on a greased cookie sheet, cover, let rise to double size. Bake at 400 degrees F for 12 to 15 minutes until buns are golden brown. Makes 2 dozen rolls

Sticky Buns

Sticky Bun Mixture-
¼ cup brown sugar
2 tbsps. butter or margarine
1 cup corn syrup
36 pecan halves
2 tbsps. butter or margarine
½ cup brown sugar

Combine ½ cup brown sugar, 2 tbsps. butter or margarine and corn syrup in a sauce pan and heat until sticky. Spoon a tablespoon of sticky sauce into 12 greased muffin cups. Put 3 pieces of pecan in each cup. Roll out sweet dough on a floured surface, into an oblong shape. Spread dough with 2 tbsps. butter or margarine and then sprinkle on ¼ cup brown sugar. Roll dough into a long roll and cut into 12 slices. Place in muffin cups. Let rise for 45 minutes.
Bake 375 degrees F for 25 minutes.

See Sweet Rolls recipe-

Krantz (German Sweet Bread)

2 tbsps. melted butter
½ cup white sugar
5 egg yolks - beaten
5 cups flour
1 ½ cups lukewarm milk
1 pkg. dry yeast – dissolved in above milk
1 lemon – grated
½ tsp. salt

Put flour, sugar, salt and lemon rind into a large bowl, add milk and yeast. Mix batter and set in a warm place to rise until double in bulk. Beat again and let rise as before. Set in a very cool place or in fridge overnight. In the morning roll out in a rectangle and cut in strips about 2 inches wide. Braid three strips together and arrange on a greased pan. Let rise and bake at 400 degrees F for 20 minutes. Brush top with syrup made of ¼ cup sugar and 2 tbsps. water and return to oven until top becomes white. Remove from oven and cool.

Mrs. John S (Angeline) Redl -dad's aunt

Raisin Bread

5 cups flour
½ cup warm water
2 yeast pkgs.
¾ cup lukewarm milk
¼ cup sugar
2 tsps. salt
¼ cup shortening
2 eggs
2 cups raisins

Combine lukewarm milk, sugar, salt and stir to dissolve. Beat in eggs; add shortening, yeast and 2 cups of flour. Beat, stir in raisins and add remainder of flour. Knead dough until all the flour is well mixed. Put in a large greased bowl, grease top of dough and cover with a cloth. Let rise for 1 ½ hours, punch down, and then let rise again. Shape dough into a bread loaf and place in greased loaf pans, let rise for about ½ hour. Preheat oven to 400 degrees F. Bake for 35 to 40 minutes until top of loaf is golden brown.

Hot Cross Buns

1 envelope yeast
1 cup lukewarm water
1 cup milk
1 tbsp. sugar
4 cups flour
1 tsp. salt
3 eggs
½ cup raisins
1/8 cup currants
½ cup mixed peel
½ cup butter or margarine
¾ cup sugar
2 tbsps. milk
½ cup icing sugar

Soak yeast in lukewarm water and add 1 tbsp. sugar. Scald milk and cool, then add yeast mixture, flour and salt and mix well. Cream butter or margarine and sugar together in separate bowl, add 2 well beaten eggs, raisins, currants and mixed peel. Beat, and then add flour mixture and mix to make stiff dough. Knead well and place in greased bowl. When dough is double in bulk, knead again, and let rise again and then form into buns. Place in well-greased pan and let rise in a warm place. With a sharp knife cut a cross in each bun. Brush with 1 egg yolk beaten in 2 tbsps. milk. Bake for 25 minutes at 350 degrees F. While buns are still warm, glaze tops with one egg white beaten with ½ cup icing sugar.

QUICK BREADS

Pizza Dough

Dough mixture-
1 cup warm water
2 tbsps. oil
1 pkg. yeast
1 tsp. white sugar
¼ tsp. salt
4 cups flour

Mix warm water, oil, yeast, sugar and salt together, stir ingredients gently. Let stand about 10 minutes. Add ½ the flour, stirring until well mixed, and then add remainder of flour, forming a soft ball. If the dough is still sticky add more flour. Knead until soft and elastic. Let the dough rise for about 10 to 15 minutes. Prepare a pizza pan by oiling the pan. Spread the dough in the pan until dough is about ½" thick – remember the dough will rise while being cooked. This amount of dough will cover a pan size 8" x 14".

Topping-
Step 1-Spread 1 – 8 oz. can tomato paste or 1- 8 oz. can tomato soup over dough
Step 2-Sprinkle on ½ tsp. oregano
Step 3-Add meat slices of choice – ham or pepperoni or salami – or any other type of meats
Step 4-Add sliced mozzarella cheese on top of meat
Bake at 400 degrees F for 25 minutes

*can add other toppings or types of cheese of choice

Variations-
Depending on choice of favorites can add additions or substitutions – examples:
Mushrooms; olives; onions; green peppers; cooked crumbled hamburger; chopped cooked steak or chicken; bacon bits; sliced hams, salami's; and/or any kind of vegetables.

****
Easy to make, no waiting for pizza delivery!

Baked Bannock

5 ½ cups flour
3 ½ tbsps. baking powder
Pinch of salt
4 ½ tbsps. lard
3 cups flour

Mix dry ingredients. Cut lard into dry mixture using a fork. Add water gradually, mixing until thickened and dough is formed. Sprinkle flour onto table and knead dough gently until soft (add small amount flour if too sticky) Do not over work the dough. Shape and flatten with rolling pin or by hand and cut biscuits with a cookie cutter. Bake 350 degrees F for 15 to 20 minutes, checking every 4 minutes. Serves about 10 pieces – pending size (can be made into biscuit shapes or baked in a cake pan and cut when cooked and cooled)

****

My best results for a light and fluffy bannock are when I bake it in a cake pan.

Fried Bannock

3 cups flour
2 ½ tbsps. baking powder
Pinch salt
3 ½ cups cold water

Mix dry ingredients. Add small amounts of water slowly, mixing gently with fork.
Knead dough gently to make sure it is not too sticky. Sprinkle flour onto table and flatten with rolling pin or by hand, about ½" thick. Melt enough lard in pan for deep frying and, heat until hot. Cut dough into pieces and cook in hot lard. Cook about 2 minutes, turning frequently to make sure even cooking and light brown. Serve warm, serving for about 14 people (depending on sizes of pieces)

Bannock on the Stick

5 ½ cups flour
3 ½ tbsps. baking powder
Pinch of salt
4 ½ tbsps. lard
3 cups flour

Mix dry ingredients. Cut lard into dry mix with a fork. Add water and mix until dough thickened to a sticky mixture. Sprinkle flour onto table and knead gently (add small amount flour if too sticky) Shape and flatten with rolling pin or by hand. Cut, stretch and roll dough around a wooden stick and place over an open wood fire pit, gradually turning to cook and brown. Once golden brown bannock is ready to eat.

Fry Bread

1 ½ cups flour
1 tsp. baking powder
1 tbsp. butter – melted
½ cup warm milk
Pinch of salt
4 tbsps. oil

To make dough, mix all ingredients expect oil in a bowl. Knead dough until smooth and divide into four pieces. Shape each piece into a flat circle. On medium heat, heat oil in a frying pan. Fry dough rounds one at a time until brown and crisp. Makes 4

****

Fry bread is a flatbread that was cooked over a fire. Native Americans introduced it to the settlers.

Scotch Scones

2 cups flour
1 tsp. salt
5 tsps. baking powder
1/3 cup milk
2 tbsps. sugar
4 tbsps. shortening
2 eggs

Mix flour, salt, and baking powder and 1 tbsp. sugar, cut in shortening with a fork or rub with finger tips. Add beaten eggs, reserving 1 egg white for the top. Add milk and mix into soft dough. Roll out on a slightly floured board or surface to ½" thickness. Cut into circles with a cookie cutter, and then cut into quarters. Brush with egg white and sprinkle with the remaining sugar. Bake at 425 degrees F for 10 to 15 minutes. Makes 10 to 12 scones.
*cinnamon may be sprinkled on scones before baking.

Quick Drop Biscuits

1 ¾ cups flour
½ tsp. salt
3 tsps. baking powder
6 tbsps. margarine
1 cup milk

Preheat oven to 450 degrees F. Mix together flour, salt and baking powder; add margarine. Cut into flour mixture until blended. Add milk and mix until ingredients are mixed together. Do not over mix. The dough should be sticky. Grease muffin tin, and then drop dough into each cup. Cook for 12 to 15 minutes. Biscuit should be slightly golden brown.

Baking Powder Biscuit

1 ¾ cups flour
2 tbsps. sugar
1 tbsp. baking powder
3 tbsps. butter or margarine
¾ cup milk

Prepare oven to 450 degrees F. Grease a baking sheet with oil. Set aside. In a large bowl, sift together the flour, sugar and baking power. Using a pastry blender or fork, cut the butter or margarine into the flour mixture until coarse crumbs form, quickly stir in milk until a soft dough forms. On a lightly floured surface, roll out dough to a ½" thickness. Using a 2 ½" biscuit cutter cut out biscuits. Gather trimmings, re-roll and cut out more biscuits until all the dough is used. Place on prepared greased baking sheet. Bake until golden brown, about 12 to 15 minutes. Place biscuits on a wire rack to cool.

Cheese Biscuits

1 cup flour
3 tsps. baking powder
¼ tsp. salt
1 tsp. margarine
½ cup cheddar cheese – grated
½ cup milk

Mix flour baking powder and salt together, add margarine and cheese blending together until crumbly. Add milk and stir until ingredients are well mixed. On a lightly floured surface, roll out dough to a ½" thickness. Using a 2 ½" biscuit cutter cut out biscuits. Gather trimmings, re-roll and cut out more biscuits until all the dough is used. Place on prepared greased baking sheet. Bake at 450 degrees F until golden brown, about 12 to 15 minutes. Place biscuits on a wire rack to cool

Plain Dumplings

2 cups flour
1 tbsp. baking powder
½ tsp. salt
¼ tsp. pepper
1 tsp. parsley flakes - optional
1 cup milk or water

Mix flour, baking powder, salt, pepper, parsley together, add milk or water gradually about half cup at a time, mixing thoroughly. Continue to add liquid until the dough is completely mixed and sticky. When stew or soup is cooked, add one tablespoon of dough at a time on top of the stew or soup. Allow space for dumpling to rise. Cover with lid and continue to cook on medium heat. Turn dumpling over once and continue to cook until fluffy and not sticky inside.

Dumplings

1 cup flour
1 tbsp. baking powder
½ tsp. salt
½ cup milk or water
2 tsps. oil

Mix flour, baking powder, salt together. Combine milk or water and oil and add gradually at half cup at a time, mixing thoroughly. Continue to add liquid until the dough is completely mixed and sticky. Drop teaspoon of dumpling dough on top of hot soup or stew, cover and boil, then lower heat to simmer. Cook for about 12 to 15 minutes.

Fruit Dumplings

Fruit-
8 cups of canned Saskatoon's or other fruits or 4 cups Saskatoon berries
1 cup sugar – use for berries only
2 cups water

Dumpling mixture-
2 cups flour
1 tbsp. baking powder
½ tsp. salt
1 cup milk or water

Mix flour, baking powder; salt together, add milk or water gradually half cup at a time, mixing thoroughly. Continue to add liquid until the dough is completely mixed and sticky. In a large sauce pan, pour in 8 cups of canned Saskatoon's, water and heat to a boil. Add one tablespoon of dough at a time on top of fruit. Cover fruit with lid and continue to cook on medium heat. Turn dumpling over once and continue to cook until fluffy and not sticky inside. Serve hot with topping of ice cream or whipped cream.
*if not using canned Saskatoon's; bring water to boil, add sugar and fruit, bring to a boil, until fruit is well cooked.

DOUGHNUTS

Doughnuts – Cake Type

3 tbsps. butter or margarine
1 cup sugar
1 tsp. vanilla
2 eggs
3 cups flour
4 tsps. baking powder
½ tsp. salt
¼ tsp. nutmeg or mace
2/3 cup milk

Cream butter or margarine and sugar together until smooth, stir in vanilla. Beat in eggs one at a time, add the dry ingredients to the mixture and mix well. Chill for 30 minutes. Roll dough out on a floured surface and cut with a doughnut cutter. Heat oil in deep fryer, and when oil is hot, drop in each doughnut, cooking until golden brown. Turn over once. Place doughnuts on a paper towel to drain oil off. Makes 1 ½ dozen doughnuts

Doughnuts – Yeast Type

4 cups milk
1 cup sugar
1 cup lard
2 yeast – pkgs.
1 ½ cups lukewarm water
1/3 cup sugar
5 eggs
1 tsp. vanilla
1 tsp. salt
4 cups flour

Boil milk, till a scum forms, add sugar and lard to milk, stir well. Let milk mixture cool. Mix yeast with lukewarm water and sugar. Then pour yeast mixture into milk. Beat eggs yolks in a separate bowl, add vanilla and salt. Pour egg mixture into the milk mixture and add flour, 1 cup at a time, mixing thoroughly, to make soft dough. Rub margarine on dough and let rise once, then knead briefly, let rise a second time. On a floured surface roll out dough, about 1 ½" thick. Cut with a doughnut cutter. Prepare to deep fry in oil.

Emily and Matthew in Grandma's kitchen making doughnuts.

Doughnuts

2 cups milk
2 cups margarine
2 tsps. salt
2 cups sugar
6 eggs
2 tbsps. vanilla
4 cups warm water
1 cup warm water
2 pkgs. fast rising yeast
2 tsps. sugar
Flour

Scald milk, margarine, salt and sugar together. Let cool to lukewarm. Add yeast, sugar and warm water, let stand for 10 minutes. In separate bowl beat 6 eggs, add 2 tsps. vanilla and 4 cups warm water. Add milk mixture and then add enough sifted flour to make a soft batter; beat well. Then add more flour to make soft dough. Let rise until double in bulk, punch down and let rise again. Roll and make doughnuts with a doughnut cutter, let rise until double in size and deep fry in oil.
*if a doughnut cutter is not available use a drinking glass or cup the same size as a doughnut cutter would be. For the center use a small round lid or something that will make a small cut. Be creative.
Makes about 10 dozen – VERY GOOD

****

Writing these doughnut recipes reminds me of the early days when I was raising my family. Everybody liked doughnuts. Who could turn them down? Making doughnuts was an all-day process, rolling out dough and making doughnuts and doughnuts. My kitchen looked like a doughnut factory. There were piles of doughnuts on the countertop and on the kitchen table. It seemed at lot until the children arrived home from school. The pile soon depleted.

I would go visit my mom and guess what? It was doughnut day, and she had piles of doughnuts spread on the kitchen table. Everybody loved doughnuts even at Grandma Wurst's.

Spud nuts -Potato Doughnuts

3 eggs
¾ cup sugar
3 tsps. shortening
2 ¾ cups flour
4 tsps. baking powder
1 tsp. salt
¼ tsp. nutmeg
1 tsp. mace
1 cup mashed cooked potatoes
1 tsp. vanilla

Mix together all ingredients then add flour to make the dough a soft texture not sticky. Chill for 2 hours. Roll dough onto a floured surface about 1" thick. Cut with doughnut cutter. Heat oil in deep fryer, and when oil is hot, drop in each doughnut, cooking until golden brown. Turning over once. Place doughnuts on a paper towel to drain oil off. Dipping into sugar or cinnamon sugar mix or icing sugar if desired.

****

My first taste of spud nuts was at my mother-in-law's, Betty Ireland. I had never heard of them before, and thought this was an inventive way to make doughnuts out of potatoes. Who would have thought a spud nut would taste so good?

Spud nuts

1 cup warm milk
½ tsp. salt
1 tbsp. yeast in ¾ cup warm water to dissolve
1 egg – well beaten
4 cups flour
½ cup hot mashed potatoes
2 tbsps. shortening
½ cup sugar
½ tsp. vanilla

Mix all ingredients together and let rise twice, and then roll out thinner than other doughnuts and cut. When slightly risen, deep fry, cool and dip in glaze.

See Spud nuts Glaze recipe-

Eggless Potato Doughnuts

2 cups cooked mashed potatoes
2 cups sugar
1 cup milk
2 tbsps. butter or margarine
5 tsps. baking powder
1 tsp. vanilla
Flour

Mix together all ingredients; add enough flour to make the dough a soft texture. Roll dough onto a floured surface to about 1" thick. Cut with doughnut cutter. Heat oil in deep fryer and when oil is hot drop in each doughnut, cooking until golden brown. Turning over once. Place doughnuts on a paper towel to drain oil off. Dip into sugar or cinnamon sugar mix, or icing sugar if desired
*potatoes keep the doughnut soft

PIES – PASTRIES

Crumb Crusts

Many pies are made with a crumb crust. Directions as follows.

Kind	Crumbs	Sugar	Butter
Graham Wafers	1 ¼ cups	2 tbsp.	1/3 cup-melted
Vanilla Wafers (24)	1 ½ cups	2 tbsps.	6 tbsps.
Ginger Snaps (18)	1 ¼ cups	1 tbsp.	1/3 cup
Cornflakes (4 cups)	1 cup	¼ cup	1/3 cup-melted
Nuts, Ground	2 cups	6 tbsp.	3 tbsps. melted
Bread Crumbs	1 1/3 cups	4 tbsps.	½ cup melted
Chocolate Wafers (18)	1 1/3 cups	1 tbsp.	3 tbsps. melted

*Unless otherwise specified, use softened butter. Combine crumbs, sugar and butter together until crumbly. Set aside 3 tbsps. for topping. Press remainder into bottom and sides of 9" pie plate, forming small rim. Bake at 375 degrees F for 10 minutes until brown. Cool and fill with favorite pie filling.
-can use margarine instead of butter.

Perfect Pie Crust

2 cups flour
½ tsp. salt
1 tbsp. sugar
¾ cup vegetable shortening
1 large egg - lightly beaten
1 tsp. vinegar
3 to 4 tbsps. cold water

Combine flour, salt and sugar in a two quart bowl. Evenly cut shortening into flour mixture with a pastry blender. Combine egg and vinegar in small bowl and add to flour mixture. Add water a tablespoon at a time until dough is moist enough to form a ball. Shape dough into 2 balls. Flatten 1 ball to ½" thickness, rounding and smoothing edges. On lightly floured surface roll into 12" circle. Fold pastry in half and place in 9" pie plate. Unfold gently and press in bottom and on sides of plate. Roll out remaining pastry, set aside.
Yields 1 – 9" double crust pie shell

Rich Flaky Pastry

2 cups flour
½ tsp. salt
¼ tsp. baking powder
2 tbsps. sugar
¼ cup lard
¼ cup butter or margarine
About 9 tablespoons of ice cold water

Stir flour, salt, baking powder and sugar together. Cut in lard and butter or margarine with pastry blender until mixture is crumbly. Add water, a little bit at a time, using just enough to bind mixture so that dough can be patted lightly to form a ball. HANDLE AS LITTLE AS POSSIBLE.

Standard Pastry

1 ½ cups flour
½ tsp. salt
½ tsp. baking powder
½ cup shortening
1/3 cup ice-cold water

Mix flour, salt and baking powder together. Cut in shortening with a pastry blender until crumbly; add water a little at a time, using just enough to bind the mixture so that dough can be patted lightly to form a ball. Ready to be rolled out on a floured surface.

****

This recipe is the one, I have used many times.

Graham Cracker Crust

1 ½ cups graham cracker crumbs
1 tsp. flour
¼ cup melted margarine or butter
2 tsps. sugar

Combine all ingredients. Press firmly into buttered 9" pie plate, making the layer uniform thickness on bottom and sides. Bake at 325 degrees F for 10 minutes. Let chill at least 45 minutes before filling. Pour in pre-cooked pie filling.

Saskatoon Pie

Fruit Filling-
3 to 3 ½ cups Saskatoon fruit
¾ to 1 cup sugar
1 tsp. lemon juice
¼ cup flour
1/8 tsp. salt
1 tbsp. butter or margarine

Wash berries thoroughly, drain and pile berries into pastry shell, piling higher in center. Combine sugar (amount will depend on sweetness of berries) flour, salt and sprinkle over berries. Sprinkle lemon juice on top and dot with butter or margarine. Cover with top crust, making slits to allow steam to escape. Seal edges and flute by pressing down with a fork. Bake at 400 degrees F for 40 to 50 minutes or until pastry is golden brown.

See Perfect Pie Crust recipe-

Strawberry Chiffon Pie

Graham Cracker Crust-
To make crust combine 1 ½ cups (10) crackers rolled to fine crumbs with ¼ cup sugar and ½ cup melted butter or margarine. Mix well and press firmly into greased 9" pie plate. Bake at 375 degrees F about 8 minutes, or until slightly browned around the edges. Cool

Filling-
To make filling, crush 1 ¼ cups strawberries and cover with ½ cup sugar. Let stand for 30 minutes. Soften 1 envelope unflavored gelatin in ¼ cup cold water and then dissolve in ½ cup of water. Cool. Add strawberries, 1 tbsp. lemon juice, and dash of salt and chill till mixture forms mound and is jelled when spooned. Fold in ½ cup whipped cream. In separate bowl beat 2 egg white and gradually beat into ¼ cup sugar until stiff peaks form. Fold into strawberry mixture, pour into crust, and chill until firm. Top with more whipped cream and berries.

****

A recipe from the Wakaw Jubilee Cookbook – the community where my dad grew up.

Flapper Pie

Custard Filling-
½ cup sugar
4 cups milk
4 eggs – separated
2 tsps. vanilla extract
3 tbsps. cornstarch

Meringue-
4 egg whites
¼ cup white sugar

Graham Cracker Crumb -
Combine the graham cracker crumbs with the sugar and softened butter or margarine and press into a 9" pie plate. Reserve a small amount of the crumbs if desired to garnish top of pie later. Bake for 5 to 7 minutes at 350 degrees F.

Filling-
Mix sugar with 3 cups of cold milk and cook in a saucepan over medium heat bringing to a boil. Stir constantly so mixture does not burn. In a separate bowl, mix 4 egg yolks, the remaining cup of milk and cornstarch and whisk the mixture until it becomes smooth. Add mixture gradually to the hot milk mixture slowly; continue stirring until the milk mixture comes to a boil or until the custard is thickened add vanilla and stir. Pour the filling over the baked crust and cool, before putting meringue on top.

Meringue Topping-
Whisk the 4 egg whites with the sugar until soft fluffy peaks form. Can use an egg beater. Spoon over the top of the pie. If desired, sprinkle extra graham cracker crumbs on top of the meringue, and cook the pie at high heat of 500 degrees F for 5 minutes or less, watching carefully so it doesn't burn. Remove from the oven when the tips of the meringue are golden.

Jim, boast about eating flapper pie, when he was working at a construction camp. He had first tasted flapper pie prepared by a local young famous chef, Harvey Steffen, who started his career, cooking in camps. Jim told me, when the guys came into camp after work, late in the evening, Harvey would have a flapper pie ready for them. The chef knew that they would appreciate his special flapper pie and they did! Flapper pie was always a topic of conversation, between Jim and his co-workers. I searched for quite a long time to find a pie recipe, similar to the one Harvey had made. And after eating Flapper Pie, I know now, why the men all sounded like happy campers when they tell the story about Flapper Pie, because this pie is delicious!

Rhubarb Pie

2 cups rhubarb – cut in small pieces
1 cup sugar
2 tbsps. flour
1 egg – unbeaten

Combine sugar, flour and egg, add to rhubarb. Mix well. Prepare pastry and line a 9" pie plate, reserving some pastry for the top crust. Add rhubarb mixture and cover with top crust, seal and flute edges with a fork. Make slits in top crust to allow steam to escape. If desired, can make a lattice top with top crust. Bake at 450 degrees F for 10 minutes, and then reduce heat to 350 degrees F for 40 to 50 minutes until rhubarb is cooked and pastry golden brown.

Traditional Pumpkin Pie

2 eggs
½ can or 2 cups of E.D. Smith Pure Pumpkin
1 cup packed brown sugar
1 tsp. ground cinnamon
½ tsp. ground nutmeg
¼ tsp. ground ginger
¼ tsp. salt
¾ cup evaporated milk
1 – 9" pie shell

Beat eggs lightly in medium bowl; add pumpkin, sugar, cinnamon, ginger, nutmeg and salt until well combined. Blend in milk. Pour filling in pie shell. Bake at 425 degrees F for 15 minutes, reduce oven temperature to 350 degrees F and continue to baking 30 to 35 minutes or until knife inserted in center comes out clean. Cool. Makes 1 pie, serves 8.

Deep Apple Pie

6 to 8 apples – peeled and cored
¾ cup sugar
½ tsp. cinnamon
2 tbsps. margarine

Peel, core and slice apples; place in 9" deep baking dish. Sprinkle with sugar and cinnamon, dot with margarine. Place prepared pastry over apples, bringing edges just over the sides of dish. Press dough on edge and flute. Make several slits on top to allow steam to escape. Bake at 450 degrees F for 10 minutes then reduce temperature to 350 degrees F and continue baking 50 to 60 minutes or until apples are done and crust is golden brown. Place on a wire rack to cool for 30 minutes. Serve warm
*serve with ice cream - alamode

CAKES – COOKIES – SQUARES – MUFFINS

Great Granny Ireland's Spice Cake

1 cup brown sugar
½ cup shortening
1 egg
¾ cup sour cream or buttermilk
1 tsp. soda
1 tsp. cinnamon
½ tsp. nutmeg
1 tsp. pastry spice or ½ tsp. allspice
1 cup raisins – optional
½ cup peel – optional
1 ½ cups flour

Mix all the ingredients together. Bake in moderate 350 degree F oven for about 25 minutes or until done.
*ice with juice of one orange and ½ cup white sugar. Blend together.
Spread on cake as soon as taken from the oven or can use an Almond Paste.

Ethel Ireland of Moosomin, Sask.

See Almond Paste recipe-

****

One fall season, Jim was hauling grain for a farmer up Weberville road. The wife heard that Jim's family came from the same community of Moosomin, Saskatchewan as she did. So, she rushed back to the house and ripped great granny Ireland's spice cake recipe from her cook book and brought it out to the field where Jim was working. She took no time to write it out. What a way to be handed a piece of family history!

****

I use this recipe at Christmas time. In 1997, at our son Stephen's wedding, Great Granny Ireland's spice cake was made as a traditional piece of wedding cake wrapped in colored foil and ribbon, and a piece was given to each wedding guest.

Carrot Cake

2 cups flour
2 cups sugar
2 tsps. baking powder
½ tsp. salt
2 tsps. cinnamon
1 tsp. allspice
1 cup rapeseed oil
4 eggs
3 cups chopped carrots –grated

Sift dry ingredients together, add oil and stir well (mixture will be very thick). Add eggs, one at a time, mixing after each addition. Add carrots and blend well. Pour batter into greased 9" x 13" pan and spread evenly. Bake 40 to 50 minutes at 350 degrees F. When cool, frost with your favorite cream cheese icing.
Double recipe – makes 3 loafs

Sugarless Date Cake

1 lb. of dates
2 tsps. baking soda
3 cups water
1 orange – chopped optional
¼ cup oil
3 cups whole wheat flour or 1 cup rice flour and 1 cup whole wheat flour
1 cup barley flour
2 tsps. baking powder
2 tsps. vanilla
1 cup walnuts or almonds – chopped
1 egg – optional

Mix dates, baking soda with boiling water, let stand for at least 4 hours. Add remaining ingredients and stir well. Pour into a greased 9" x 12" pan. Bake at 350 degrees F for 45 minute.

Johnny Cake

1 cup flour
3 ½ tsps. baking powder
½ tsp. salt
1 cup yellow cornmeal
1/3 cup brown sugar – packed
1 egg- well beaten
7/8 cup milk
5 tbsps. Shortening – melted

Mix flour, baking powder and salt in a bowl, mix in cornmeal and sugar. Make a well in the flour mixture for the liquids. Mix beaten egg, milk and shortening together, add to dry mixture and stir. Pour into a well-greased cake pan. Bake at 400 degrees F for 20 to 25 minutes.
Serve hot with maple syrup or maple syrup topping.

Maple Syrup Topping-

2 cups brown sugar
1 cup water
2 tbsps. Margarine
1 tsp. vanilla
1 tsp. maple flavor

Stir brown sugar into water and bring to a boil for about 5 minutes, stir in margarine, cool then stir in vanilla and maple flavorings.

****

Mom made Johnny cake often and it never really appealed to me, even with Rodgers syrup drizzled over the top. It was one of these cakes her mother made for them, and which is an American recipe. My grandmother always said, "she was American, and proud of it".

41

Molasses cake

½ cup margarine
1 ½ cups sugar
2 eggs - well beaten
3 cups flour
4 tsps. baking powder
1 cup milk
1 tsp. vanilla
¼ tsp. salt
1 cup molasses
1 cup raisins – optional

Cream margarine, sugar together until creamy, add beaten eggs, vanilla and molasses stirring together. Pour in the milk and stir. Add flour, baking powder, raisins and salt into the mixture and mix until the batter is smooth. Pour into a greased 9" x 13" cake pan. Bake at 350 degrees F for 35 to 40 minutes, until golden brown.

Tomato Soup Cake

1 ½ cups brown or ½ cup white sugar
½ cup shortening
2 eggs
1 ¾ cups flour
1 cup raisins
½ cup walnuts
1 tsp. baking soda
1 tsp. baking powder
1/8 tsp. salt
½ tsp. cinnamon
½ tsp. nutmeg
1 cup tomato soup

Mix all the ingredients together, pour into a greased pan and bake at 350 degrees F for 50 minutes.

Birthday Cake Tradition

Birthdays – a special moment of surprise when your slice of cake had something shiny in it. In days past, mom would place pennies, nickels, dimes and quarters in our birthday cakes, and everyone would be surprised at the amount of money they would find in their piece of cake.

Mom would take a handful of coins – pennies, dimes, nickels and quarters, place them in a pot of boiling water, and sterilize them, and then drop them into the cake batter. No one would know where the money was until they took a bite out of their piece of cake. We were always surprised when a coin or two showed up.

For a period of time, I followed the same tradition of placing coins into my children's birthday cakes. Then it became something not to do, the germ thing, or maybe not so cool.

Coins in birthday cakes must have been the tradition, as other families did the same. Even my husband's mother placed coins in their birthday cakes.

Egg-Yolk Sponge Cake

2 ¼ cups flour
3 tsps. baking powder
½ tsp. salt
9 egg yolks
1 ½ cups sugar
2 tsps. lemon extract
¾ cup boiling water
1 tsp. lemon rind

Heat oven to 325 degrees F. Beat together egg yolks, add sugar gradually and beat, add lemon extract and beat. Add boiling water gradually, beating constantly. Add dry ingredients and grated lemon rind and fold in quickly. Pour batter into an ungreased 10" tube pan and bake for 55 minutes or until top springs back when touched lightly. Invert pan immediately on a funnel or the neck of a soft-drink bottle. Let hang until cold.
*can use egg whites to make an angel food cake.

Devil's Food Cake

2 cups flour
½ cup cocoa
1 tsp. salt
1 tsp. baking soda
¾ cup shortening
1 ½ cup sugar
1 tsp. vanilla
2 eggs
½ cup buttermilk or sour milk
½ cup boiling water
1 tsp. red food coloring- optional

Heat oven to 350 degrees F, grease and flour two 8" round, 1 ½" deep layer cake pans. Cream shortening until fluffy, add sugar and vanilla, and continue to cream until fluffy. Add eggs one at a time and beat well after each one. Add dry ingredients alternating with buttermilk, beat well after each addition. Add boiling water and beat well again. Stir in red food coloring if desired. Bake for 35 minutes or until top springs back when touched lightly in the middle. Let stand in pans a few minutes then turn over on rack to cool. Ice with your favorite frosting or glaze.

Cocoa Ripple Ring

½ cup shortening
¾ cup sugar
1 ½ cups flour
2 eggs
¾ tsp. salt
2 tsps. baking powder
2/3 cup milk
1/3 cup instant cocoa –dry
1/3 cup walnuts – chopped
3 tbsps. margarine

Cream shortening, sugar and eggs together. Add dry ingredients to creamed mixture, pour in milk and mix well. Spoon 1/3 batter in a baking ring pan, sprinkle ½ cocoa over batter. Repeat batter layers. Let stand 5 minutes. Bake 35 minutes at 350 degrees F. Serve warm

Kaffee Kuchen

Batter-
1/2 cup butter
1 cup sugar
2 egg yolks
1 ½ cups flour
2 tsps. baking powder
½ tsp. salt
½ cup milk
2 egg whites – stiffly beaten

Cream butter and sugar together until creamy, beat in egg yolks until well mixed. Add dry ingredients and mix, add milk and mix in, fold in egg whites. Pour in a greased pan. Bake for 30 minutes at 350 degrees F.
Serve warm

Topping-
½ cup flour
¼ cup brown sugar
2 tbsps. margarine

Mix together till crumbly. Sprinkle over top of baked batter.

Plain Sponge Cake

1 cup flour
4 or 5 eggs
1 cup sugar
2 tbsps. lemon juice
1 tsp. lemon rind- grated
½ tsp. salt

Beat egg yolks until thick and lemon color. Gradually add half the sugar, beating thoroughly and then the lemon juice and rind. Beat until thick. In separate bowl beat the egg whites and salt until they start to peak but will still flow. Fold in the rest of the sugar, then the yolk mixture. Fold in flour gently. Pour the batter as soon as it is mixed, into an ungreased baking pan, for a large or medium size loaf. A tube pan is best, because the center opening allows the mixture to heat evenly. Powdered sugar sifted over top makes a more desirable crust. Bake at 300 degrees F for 50 to 60 minutes. After baked invert the cake to cool on a funnel, but remove from the pan before it is entirely cold.

Light Strawberry Cheesecake

3 tbsps. graham wafer crumbs
1 pkg. Jell-O – strawberry – lite
2/3 cup boiling water
16 oz. light Philadelphia cream cheese
2 cups semi-thawed cool whip - lite

Sprinkle graham wafer crumbs onto sides and bottom of an 8" spring form pan which has been sprayed with non-stick cooking spray or lightly oiled. Place Jell-O in a bowl and add hot water to dissolve, cool, add cream cheese, blend with a blender at medium speed until smooth, add cool whip and continue to blend until thick and smooth. Fold ingredients into a spring form pan, smooth top, chill for 4 hours. Can add decorative fruit to the top. Ready to be served

****

Strawberry Cheesecake is my favorite dessert, because it is simple and easy to make. The perfect dessert for those who love cheesecake, very light and a special dessert suitable for diabetics.

46

New British Truffle

Bake a Plain Sponge Cake-

See Plain Sponge Cake recipe-

1 plain sponge cake
Raspberries – fresh or frozen
Cream of Sherry brandy
Raspberry juice
Raspberry Jell-O
Vanilla custard
Whipping cream
Strawberries - fresh
Almonds – slivers
Cherries – red and green

Cool cake, and then cut in half, length wise, then each half cut into 8 sections. Put 4 pieces of cake on bottom of a glass pedestal bowl. Spread over layer with fresh or thawed frozen raspberries. Then pour mixed cream of sherry brandy and juice of raspberries over the fruit. Soaking the cake. Place the next 4 pieces of cake on top, fruit and repeat with sherry brandy and juice. Then repeat next 4 pieces of cake, pouring over layer with raspberry Jell-O (1/2 set) then cover with sliced strawberries and almond slivers. Place last 4 pieces of cake then pour vanilla custard over the layer, and then add whipped cream, topped with red and green cherry halves.

See Custard recipe-

Upside Down Cake

Batter-
½ cup margarine
1 ½ cups sugar
2 eggs- well beaten
3 cups flour
4 tsps. baking powder
1 cup milk
1 tsp. vanilla
¼ tsp. salt

Cream margarine, sugar together until creamy, add beaten eggs and vanilla and stir in. Pour in the milk and stir. Add flour, baking powder and salt into the mixture and mix until the batter is smooth.

Fruit Mixture-
4 cups rhubarb – cooked
½ cup sugar
1 – 3oz pkg. strawberry Jell-O
¼ cup flour

Mix fruit mixture together until well mixed. Pour into a greased 9" x 13" cake pan. Spread batter evenly over the fruit mixture. Bake at 375 degrees F for 40 to 55 minutes, until the batter is done and golden brown. Serve warm with ice cream or whipped cream.
*other fruit – Saskatoon's, Raspberries, Peaches – canned or fresh. Can omit Jell-O when using other fruits.

Angel Food Cake

1 cup cake flour
1 ¼ cups sugar
1 ½ cups egg whites – better if 3 days old
¼ tsp. salt
1 tsp. cream of tartar
1 tsp. vanilla
¼ tsp. almond extract

Sift flour once, measure, sift 3 times. Beat egg whites and salt until foaming, add cream of tartar and continue beating until eggs are stiff enough to hold peaks. Sift sugar 3 times, folding in 2 tbsps. at a time until all sugar is blended. Then fold in 2 tbsps. flour at a time until all used. Fold in flavoring. Pour into greased angel food pan. Cut through batter with knife to remove bubbles. Bake at 275 degrees F for 1 hour. Remove from oven and invert pan for one hour or until cake is cold.

****

Angel food cakes are one of the most difficult cakes to make. I found this type of cake needed to be mixed according to the directions and cooked in a special pan. For a number of years I would make angel food cakes, for birthdays, in an old well-seasoned cake pan. A bit of boasting, but my cakes never failed. However, these days we can buy a mix, or go to the store and purchase a ready-made cake. How times are changing!

Eggless - Milkless- Butterless Cake

1 cup brown sugar
1 cup raisins
1 cup water
½ cup shortening
½ tsp. salt
½ tsp. cloves
1 tsp. cinnamon
¼ tsp. nutmeg
1 tsp. baking soda
2 cups flour + 2 tsps. flour
1 tsp. baking powder

Combine sugar, raisins, water, shortening and spices in a saucepan. Boil for 3 minutes. Remove from heat and cool. Dissolve baking soda in 2 tsps. of warm water and add to boiled mixture. Sift flour and baking powder together and add to boiled mixture. Mix well and pour into a 9" x 9" greased cake pan. Bake at 375 degrees F for 30 minutes.

****

This is a great recipe to make for the kid's lunches, especially when there is not enough milk, eggs and shortening in the fridge, the store is closed, or you live a distance from town.

Pound Fruit Cake

1 ½ cups date
2 cups fruit mix
½ cup cherries
½ cup dark raisins
1 cup walnuts
1 cup flour
½ tsp. grated lemon rind
1 pkg. pound cake mix
¼ cup butter or margarine
¾ cup milk
2 eggs

Toss dates, fruit, walnuts, raisins, cherries into ½ cup flour. In separate bowl combine remaining flour, lemon and cake mix in a bowl, blend in butter or margarine, add ½ cup milk and blend in dry ingredients. Beat for 1 minute, add eggs, beat 1 minute and add milk beat 1 minute. Then stir in fruit mixture. Grease two loaf pans. Pour batter into each pan equally. Bake at 325 degrees F for 1 hour and 20 minutes. Can be frozen.

Jelly Roll

2 eggs- beaten
1 cup white sugar
3 tbsps. milk
1 cup flour
2 tsps. baking powder
¼ tsp. salt
1 tsp. vanilla or lemon extract

Mix together and pour into wax paper lined 9" x 13" pan and bake at 400 degrees F for about 12 minutes. The jelly roll should be about 2" thick when baked. When done, turn onto a clean dish cloth sprinkled with icing sugar and trim the long edge of roll. Spread with jam or lemon pie filling. Roll up on cloth and leave until set. Remove cloth and slice.

Chocolate Zucchini Cake

½ cup margarine
½ cup oil
1 ¾ cups sugar
2 eggs
½ tsp. vanilla
½ cup sour milk
2 ½ cups flour
½ tsp. salt
4 tbsps. cocoa
½ tsp. baking powder
½ tsp. baking soda
½ tsp. cinnamon
½ tsp. cloves
2 cups zucchini – grated

Cream margarine, oil and sugar together, add eggs, vanilla and sour milk. Stir mixture well. Add flour, salt, cocoa, baking powder, baking soda, cinnamon, cloves and zucchini into mixture and mix well. Pour in greased loaf pan. Bake at 350 degrees F for 50 minutes. Cool in pan for 10 minutes, remove from pan and cool completely before slicing. Makes 1 loaf.

Zucchini Gingerbread

3 eggs
4 cups flour
1 tsp. salt
1 tsp. baking powder
1 tsp. baking soda
1 tsp. ground ginger
2 cups brown sugar
½ cup oil
¼ cup molasses
2 cups zucchini- grated
1 tsp. vanilla
½ cup raisins

Mix together flour, salt, baking powder, baking soda and ginger; set aside. In a large mixing bowl combine eggs, brown sugar, oil, molasses, zucchini and vanilla. Stir in flour mixture until smooth. Fold in raisins. Pour into two well-greased loaf pans. Bake at 350 degrees F for 75 minutes or checking by inserting a knife in center of loaf, and knife comes out clean. Cool in pan for 10 minutes, remove from pan and cool completely before slicing. Makes 2 loafs.

Cinnamon Zucchini Cake

½ cup margarine
½ cup oil
1 ¾ cups sugar
2 eggs
½ tsp. vanilla
½ cup sour milk
2 ½ cups flour
½ tsp. salt
½ tsp. baking powder
½ tsp. baking soda
1 ½ tsps. cinnamon
½ tsp. cloves
½ tsp. allspice
2 cups zucchini – grated

Cream margarine, oil and sugar together, add eggs, vanilla and sour milk. Stir mixture well. Add flour, salt, baking powder, baking soda, cinnamon, cloves, allspice and zucchini into mixture and mix well. Pour in greased loaf pan. Bake at 350 degrees F for 40 to 50 minutes. Cool in pan for 10 minutes, remove from pan and cool completely before slicing.
Makes 1 loaf

Banana Bread

½ cup margarine
¾ cup sugar
2 eggs- beaten
1 cup flour
1 tsp. baking soda
½ tsp. salt
1 cup whole wheat flour –optional in place of another type of flour
3 large ripe bananas, mashed or 1 cup frozen mashed bananas
1 tsp. vanilla
½ cup walnuts- coarsely chopped

Preheat oven to 350 degrees F, grease 9" x 5" x 3" loaf pan. Cream butter and sugar until light and fluffy. Add eggs one at a time, beating well after each addition. Sift flour, baking soda and salt together, stir in whole wheat flour and add to creamed mixture, mixing well. Fold in bananas, vanilla and walnuts. Pour mixture into pan, bake 50 to 60 minutes or until testing with knife inserted in middle comes out clean. Cool in pan for 10 minutes, and then flip out onto rack. Makes 1 loaf.

Pumpkin Loaf

2 eggs –beaten
1 ½ cups sugar
1 cup pumpkin- cooked/mashed or can pumpkin
½ cup oil
¼ cup water
¼ tsp. baking powder
1 tsp. soda
¾ tsp. salt
½ tsp. cloves
½ tsp. cinnamon
1 2/3 cups flour
½ cup raisins and nuts – optional

Combine eggs and sugar. Mix well. Add pumpkin, oil and water. Add all dry ingredients and mix. Add raisins and nuts if desired. Bake in loaf pans for 1 hour at 350 degrees or in a 9" x 12" cake pan for 35 minutes at 375 degrees F.

Strawberry Shortcake

Pastry-
1 ¾ cups flour
2 tbsps. sugar
1 tbsp. baking powder
3 tbsps. butter or margarine
¾ cup milk

Filling-
4 cups fresh strawberries-sliced
1 tbsp. sugar
2 cups vanilla non-fat yogurt, cool whip or whipped cream

Prepare oven to 450 degrees F. Grease a baking sheet with oil. Set aside. In a large bowl, sift together the flour, sugar and baking powder. Using a pastry blender or fork, cut the butter or margarine into the flour mixture until coarse crumbs form, quickly stir in milk until a soft dough forms. On a lightly floured surface, roll out dough to a ½" thickness. Using a 2 ½" biscuit cutter cut out biscuits. Gather trimmings, re-roll, and cut out more biscuits until all the dough is used. Place on prepared baking sheet. Bake until golden brown, about 12 to 15 minutes. Place biscuits on a wire rack to cool.

To prepare filling, in a large bowl, combine strawberries and sugar. Mix well. Split warm biscuits in half horizontally. Place bottom halves on serving plate. Top each with some filling. Cover with biscuit tops. Add remaining filling on top of the biscuit with whipped cream.
Serves 8

Rice Krispie Squares

½ cup margarine
250 g. pkg. large marshmallows
5 cups rice crispy cereal

In large heavy saucepan, melt margarine, add marshmallows and melt over low heat, stirring until they are completely melted. Fill a large bowl with Rice Krispie cereal and then pour the melted marshmallows over the cereal, mixing until all the cereal is well coated. Press into a greased 8" x 8" pan. Let stand until cool, and then cut into squares.

****

Is there a child that doesn't like Rice Krispie Squares and asks for more? This is one of the favorites in our home.

Puff Wheat Squares

1/3 cup margarine
1/3 cup corn syrup
½ cup brown sugar
1 ½ tbsps. cocoa
6 cups puffed wheat

Combine margarine, syrup, sugar and cocoa in saucepan. Stir and bring to a boil for about 5 minutes and then do a cold water dip. (take a teaspoon of syrup mixture and dip into a glass of cold water to check syrup formation, which should form a soft toffee ball). Fill a large bowl with 6 cups of puffed wheat. Pour boiled mixture over the puffed wheat, mixing until well coated. Press evenly in a greased 8" x 8" pan. Cool. Cut into squares.

Nanaimo Bars

Bottom Layer-
½ cup butter or margarine
¼ cup sugar
5 tbsps. cocoa
1 egg- beaten
1 ¾ cups graham wafer crumbs
1 cup fine coconut
½ cup chopped walnuts

Melt first three ingredients in top of double boiler or in a heavy saucepan. Add egg, stir to cook and thicken. Remove from heat. Stir in crumbs, coconut and nuts. Press firmly into ungreased 9" x 9" pan.

Second Layer-
½ cup margarine
3 tbsps. milk
2 tbsps. vanilla custard powder
2 cups icing sugar

Cream margarine, milk, custard powder and icing sugar together well. Beat until light, spread over bottom layer.

Third Layer-
2/3 cup semi-sweet chocolate chips or 4 squares of chocolate (1 oz. each)
2 tbsps. margarine

Melt chips and margarine over low heat. Cool. When cool but still runny, spread over second layer. Chill in refrigerator. Use a sharp knife to cut into squares.

Matrimonial Squares

Crumb Layer-
1 ¼ cups flour
1 ½ cups rolled oats
1 cup brown sugar- packed
1 tsp. baking soda
½ tsp. salt
1 cup margarine

Measure flour, oats, sugar, baking soda, salt and margarine into large bowl. Mix margarine into the ingredients until crumbly. Press three quarters of crumbs into greased 9" x 9" pan.

Filling-
½ lb. dates- cut up
½ cup sugar
2/3 cup water or more if needed

In saucepan combine dates, sugar and water. Bring to boil and allow to simmer until mushy. If mixture becomes too dry before dates have softened enough, add more water. If you find you have too much water, don't worry. Just keep simmering until some has been boiled away. Spread over bottom crumbs, sprinkle remaining crumbs over the top covering the filling mix. Press down with your hand. Bake at 350 degrees F for 30 minutes until a rich golden brown color. Makes 36 squares.

Butterscotch Delight

1 – 12 oz. pkg. butterscotch chips
½ cup peanut butter
1 tsp. vanilla
1/3 cup butter or margarine
1/3 cup coconut
Pinch of salt
½ pkg. miniature marshmallows

Melt and stir chips and margarine over low heat. Stir in other ingredients until well blended. Add miniature marshmallows. Spread in an 8" square pan. Cool

Dream Bars 1

1 stick margarine
1 ½ cups flour
1 cup brown sugar
1 cup pecans – toasted
6 tbsps. margarine
3 eggs
1 tsp. vanilla
½ tsp. baking powder
¼ tsp. salt
1 ½ cups coconut flakes – unsweetened
14 oz. sweetened condensed milk

Line a 9" x 13" pan with foil, coat with margarine. In a bowl combine 1 cup flour, ½ cup brown sugar and pecans. Work in margarine, rubbing mixture until crumbly. Lightly pat onto bottom of pan. Set aside. In mixing bowl beat eggs and remaining brown sugar together then add vanilla, continue to beat. In another bowl sift together remaining flour, baking powder and salt, stir into egg mixture. Spread mixture on top of bottom layer. Sprinkle on coconut and then pour on sweetened condensed milk. Bake at 350 degrees F for 25 to 30 minute until the tiny bubbles show and top turns golden brown. Set on a rack to cool. Run a knife along the edges of the foil pan sides to loosen, and then lift whole cake out of the pan. Cut into 2" bars.

Dream Bar 2

Base-
½ cup shortening
½ cup brown sugar
1 cup flour

Mix shortening, sugar together to a creamy texture. Add flour, stir until crumbly mix. Flatten into bottom of ungreased pan. Bake for 10 minutes at 350 degrees F.

Topping-
2 eggs
1 cup brown sugar
1 tsp. vanilla
2 tsps. flour
1 tsp. baking powder
½ tsp. salt
1 cup coconut
1 cup nuts

Mix all the ingredients together and spread over the base mixture. Bake for 25 minutes at 350 degrees F. Cool and cut into bars.

Chocolate Chip and Walnut Squares

½ cup margarine
1 ½ cups graham wafers
1 cup shredded coconut
1 small pkg. chocolate chips
1 can sweetened condensed milk
1 cup chopped nuts

Preheat oven to 350 degrees F. Use a 9" x 13" pan. Melt margarine in sauce pan. Mix margarine and graham wafer crumbs together and spread evenly in baking pan. Place an even layer of coconut. Sprinkle chocolate chips over coconut. Pour sweetened condensed milk over and top with chopped nuts. Do not stir. Bake for 35 to 40 minutes. Cool completely before slicing.

Caramel Slices

¼ cup margarine
1 cup brown sugar – packed
1 egg
½ cup walnuts – chopped
¾ cup flour
1 tsp. baking powder
¼ tsp. salt
1 cup coconut – medium shredded

Melt margarine in large saucepan. Remove from heat. Add sugar, stir, and then add beaten egg. Measure in nuts, flour, baking powder, salt and coconut. Stir well. Spoon into greased 9" x 9" pan. Bake at 350 degrees F for 30 minutes or until set and a medium brown. Frost when cool with caramel icing.

Caramel Icing-
¼ cup margarine
½ cup brown sugar
2 tbsps. milk
1 cup icing sugar

Combine margarine and brown sugar in saucepan. Add milk and bring to a boil. Simmer for 2 minutes. Cool. Add icing sugar and beat. If too stiff, add a bit more of milk until soft enough to spread. Smooth over bars. Cut when set. Yields 36 squares.

Skor Bars

1 box Ritz original cracker – small box
1 can Eagle Brand milk – the light does not work as well
1 bag Skor chips

Crush crackers in processor or blender or use a rolling pin. Add eagle brand milk and Skor Chips less ¼ cup. Mix well and press into a 9" x 13" greased pan .Bake for 10 minutes at 350 degrees F. Cool and ice with Philadelphia Cream Cheese Icing. Sprinkle top with ¼ cup of Skor Chips.

See Philadelphia Cream Cheese Icing recipe-

Date Squares

Pastry mixture-
1 cup flour
1 tsp. baking soda
1 cup brown sugar- packed
2 cups rolled oats
¾ cup soft shortening

Sift flour, baking soda and brown sugar together. Add rolled oats and soft shortening; combined thoroughly. Spread half of this mixture in a greased pan. Pat down lightly.

Filling-
2 cups chopped dates
1/3 cup brown sugar – packed
1 ¼ cups water
1 tbsp. flour
1 tsp. vanilla

Combine dates, brown sugar, water and flour and cook until thickened, stirring constantly. Cool, and then add vanilla. Spread filling evenly over pastry mixture; cover with remaining pastry and pat down. Bake at 375 degrees F for 20 minutes. Cut in squares when cool.

Polynesian Treat

Bring 1 cup crushed pineapple, 1 tsp. vanilla and 2 to 3 drops yellow food coloring, to a boil in sauce pan. Remove from heat; add 3 cups marshmallows and ½ cup nuts. Stir until marshmallows melt. Chill until thickened. Chill 2/3 cups milk in refrigerator ice tray until soft ice crystals form. Then whip until stiff, add 1 tbsp. lemon juice, and fold in marshmallows mixture. In separate bowl mix 2 cups crushed ginger snap cookies with 1/3 cup margarine. Press ½ of crumb mixture in bottom of pan, spread ½ marshmallow mixture over crumbs, repeat layer of crumbs and mixture. Chill 2 to 3 hours.
Serves 8

Midnight Mints

Bottom Layer-
½ cup butter or margarine
5 tbsps. cocoa
¼ cup sugar
1 egg –beaten
2 cups graham wafer crumbs
½ cup walnuts – chopped
1 cup shredded coconut

Combine margarine, cocoa and sugar in a sauce pan. Bring slowly to a boil; stir in egg to thicken; Remove from heat and add crumbs, coconut and walnuts, mixing together and press down in a greased pan.

Second Layer-
½ cup margarine
3 tbsps. milk
1 tsp. peppermint flavor
2 cups icing sugar
Sprinkle of green food coloring

Combine ingredients together in a bowl. Mix well and add more liquid if needed. Add green food coloring, blend in and spread over the first layer.

Third Layer-
2/3 cup chocolate chips
2 tbsps. margarine

Melt chips and margarine in a sauce pan over low heat. Stir well and pour over second layer. Chill and store in refrigerator. Will keep well and can be frozen. Makes 36 square

Butter Tart Squares

Bottom Layer-
1 ¼ cups flour
½ cup butter
¼ cup brown sugar

Mix together and press mixture in a 9" square pan. Bake at 350 degrees F for 15 minutes.

Top Layer-
1/3 cup butter
2 tbsps. cream
1 tsp. vanilla
1 cup raisins
1 cup brown sugar
1 egg – beaten
1 tbsp. flour

Mix together and spread over base. Return to oven and bake for 20 to 30 minutes or until golden brown.

Prize Butter Tarts

Filling-
2 eggs - beaten
2/3 cup butter
2 cups brown sugar
3 tbsps. milk
1 cup raisins or currants or pecans
2 tsps. vanilla
1 pastry recipe

Prepare pastry; roll 1/8" thick and cut in 4" rounds. Press into medium-size tart pan. Mix filling ingredients together until smooth and creamy. Fill tart shells 2/3 full. Bake at 350 degrees F for 20 to 25 minutes or until pastry is golden brown. Yields 2 dozen

See Pastry recipe-

Quick Shortbread

½ cup icing sugar
½ cup butter
2 cups flour and pinch salt
½ tsp. almond extract
½ tsp. vanilla extract

Cream butter; add sugar, then flour, salt and flavorings. Mix with mix-master until smooth. Drop by tablespoon onto cookie sheet, press with fork and top with a cherry (red or green) or walnut. Bake at 350 degrees F for 20 to 30 minutes.

Shortbread

2 cups flour
1 cup butter – soft
½ cup icing sugar

Mix butter until creamy, add icing sugar until mixture is well blended and smooth. Add flour gradually, ½ cup at a time, stir until all flour is well mixed in. On a floured board take the dough and roll it back and forth gently until the mixture is soft and flexible. Do not over knead. Spread dough, about 2 ½" thick on an ungreased cookie sheet. Use a fork to make prints on the dough. Bake at 350 degrees F for about 20 minutes or until light brown.

Auntie Edith Hall

****

Scottish Shortbread
Betty Ireland always said "never cut shortbread, break into pieces"
-Brings Good Luck-

66

Shortbread
For Diabetics

½ lb. soft butter
½ cup icing sugar
½ cup rice flour
1 ¾ cups flour

Cream butter and icing sugar in a mixing bowl until soft and fluffy. Stir in flours until well blended. Roll the dough into a ball and place on a floured surface and continue to mix and roll until the dough is soft and not breaking apart. Do not over knead. Place in an ungreased pan, about 2" thick. Prick with a fork to form designs. Bake at 325 degrees F for 22 to 25 minutes or until golden brown. Should make 60 pieces, pending on size when breaking off pieces.

Raspberry Bars

Bottom Layer-
1 ¼ cups flour
½ cup margarine
¼ cup sugar

Combine all ingredients in bowl. Mix together until crumbly. Press into a greased 9"x 9" pan.

Filling-
1 cup raspberry jam

Spread jam over bottom layer.

Top Layer-
2 eggs
1 cup sugar
2 cups coconut- shredded
1 tsp. vanilla
½ tsp. baking powder

Beat eggs until frothy. Add sugar, coconut, vanilla and baking powder. Stir to combine well. Spread over jam layer. Bake at 350 degrees F for 30 minutes or until set and lightly browned. Cool and cut into 36 squares

Raspberry Squares

1 cup flour
1 tbsp. milk
1 egg
½ tsp. salt
1 tsp. baking powder
½ cup butter or margarine

Mix these ingredients together like pie dough and roll out to fit a 9" x 12" pan. Spread a thin layer of raspberry jam on top of dough.

Filling-
1 cup white sugar
¼ cup butter or margarine – melted
1 tsp. vanilla
1 ½ cups coconut
1 egg- beaten

Mix ingredients well and spread over jam. Bake at 350 degrees F for 25 minutes. Cut in squares while warm.

Ginger Snaps

2 cups brown sugar
2 eggs
1 tsp. nutmeg
1 tbsp. baking soda
3 ½ cups flour
1 cup shortening
1 cup molasses
2 tbsps. ginger

Cream shortening, add sugar and beat well. Add one egg at a time and keep beating. Add molasses, nutmeg and ginger. Sift baking soda with flour and add to first mixture. Mix well. Roll into balls the size of a walnut, place on a greased cookie sheet. Bake at 350 degrees F for about 10 minutes.

Tropical Bars

Bottom layer-
1 cup flour
¼ tsp. salt
¼ cup margarine
¼ cup brown sugar

Mix together and pat into pan. Bake at 325 degrees F for 15 minutes.

Filling-
1 egg- beaten
1 cup brown sugar
½ cup crushed pineapple
1 cup coconut
¼ cup chopped cherries
1 tsp. rum flavor
½ cup flour
1 tsp. baking powder

Mix together and pour batter on top of base mixture. Bake for 30 to 35 minutes at 325 degrees F.

Caramel Toffee Squares

Bottom Layer-
½ cup plus 2 tsps. margarine
¼ cup sugar
1 ¼ cups flour

Mix ingredients together until crumbly. Pat into ungreased 9" x 9" pan. Bake at 350 degrees F for 20 minutes.

Second Layer-
½ cup margarine
½ cup brown sugar – packed
2 tbsps. corn syrup
½ cup sweetened condensed milk – not evaporated

Combine margarine, sugar, syrup and milk in saucepan. Bring to boil and continue to boil for 5 minutes. Remove from heat. Beat and pour over bottom layer.

Third Layer-
1 pkg. 12 oz. semi-sweet chocolate chips

Melt chocolate in saucepan over low heat. Pour over second layer. Cool. Cut into 36 squares.

Soft Molasses Cookies

1 cup molasses
1 cup sugar
1 cup melted margarine
1 cup sour milk
2 beaten eggs
4 cups flour
1 ½ cups raisins – optional
1 tsp. ginger
1 tsp. cinnamon
1 tsp. soda
3 tsps. baking powder
½ tsp. salt

Mix together first 3 ingredients thoroughly. Add spices and salt. Dissolve soda in 2 tbsp. cold water and add eggs. Add milk and stir. Add flour, raisins and baking powder. Mix together until cookie dough is well mixed. Drop on greased cookie sheet. Bake at 375 degrees F for about 10 minutes or until done.

Molasses Spice Cookies

1 ¼ cups whole wheat flour
1 tsp. baking soda
½ tsp. cinnamon
½ tsp. ground ginger
½ tsp. ground cloves
6 tbsps. butter – softened
1 egg
2 tbsps. molasses
1 tbsp. vanilla extract
½ cup date sugar
¼ cup currants

Sift flour, baking soda, cinnamon, ginger and cloves together in a large bowl. In a second large bowl, beat butter, egg, molasses, vanilla and date sugar together until thoroughly blended. Add currants, and stir in the flour mixture until all is thoroughly blended. With floured hands form the dough into balls about 1" in diameter and arrange them 1" apart on a greased cookie sheets. Bake at 375 degrees F for about 12 minutes or until the cookies are puffed and cracks show on top. Cool on wire racks.
Makes 2 dozen cookies.

Coconut Crisp Cookies

2 cups brown sugar
1 cup shortening
2 eggs
1 tsp. baking powder
½ tsp. baking soda
2 cups flour
2 cups oatmeal
2 cups coconut

Cream sugar and shortening, add eggs, then dry ingredients. Roll mixture into small balls and place on a greased cookie sheet. Press each ball down with a fork. Bake at 400 degrees F for 10 to 12 minutes

Coconut Macaroons

2 egg whites
¼ tsp. cream of tartar
1 cup white sugar
1 tbsp. cornstarch
1 tsp. vanilla
2 cups coconut

Place egg whites, cream of tartar and white sugar in double boiler and beat over heat with egg beater until stiff. Take off heat and add the cornstarch, vanilla and coconut. Stir. Drop by spoonful on cookie sheet. Decorate with small pieces of green and red maraschino cherries and bake in slow oven at 325 degrees F for 8 minutes or until slightly brown.
Makes 25 cookies

Coconut Cookies

½ cup butter
1 ¼ cups sugar
2 eggs
½ tsp. salt
1 tsp. baking soda
2 cups flour
1 cup coconut
1 tsp. vanilla

Sift together flour, baking soda and salt, set aside. Cream together butter and sugar until soft and fluffy. Add in beaten eggs, vanilla and stir. Add coconut and mix. Stir in dry ingredients and mix well. Drop cookies on greased cookie sheet and bake at 350 degrees F for 10 to 12 minutes.

Monster Cookies

6 eggs
2 cups brown sugar
2 cups white sugar
1 tbsp. vanilla
½ lb. butter
3 cups peanut butter
1 tbsp. syrup
9 cups oatmeal
½ cup chocolate chipits
2 cups Smarties
4 tsps. baking soda
1 tsp. salt

Combine all ingredients together, mixing well. Drop by teaspoonful onto a greased cookie sheet. Bake at 350 degrees F for 10 minutes.

Oat Delight- No Bake Cookies

2 cups brown sugar
6 tbsps. cocoa
½ cup margarine
½ cup milk
½ tsp. vanilla
1 cup shredded coconut- optional
3 cups rolled oats

Combine sugar, cocoa, margarine and milk in saucepan; bring to a boil until liquid bubbles and spoon makes an indented track through liquid, continue to boil for about 5 minutes. Add vanilla. Remove from heat and stir in coconut and rolled oats. Quickly, drop by teaspoonful onto wax paper; chill
Makes 4 ½ dozen.

****

This is a quick and easy recipe to make for school lunches. My family liked these a lot, and I never had to worry about too many left in the cookie tin. My little munchkin's made sure they didn't even get to the cookie tin.

****

As a youngster, Jamie-Anne was the cookie maker in our house. She loved to bake cookies of all kinds. Her first few attempts were trial runs, because she may not have completely mixed the ingredients together well enough, or added too much baking powder or salt. However, over time her baking skills improved and the cookies were always appreciated and delicious.
Jamie-Anne tells me that her favorite cookie to make was the Oat Delight- No Bake Cookie.

Crackerjack Cookies

1 cup margarine
1 cup brown sugar
1 cup white sugar
2 eggs
1 ½ tsps. vanilla
1 ½ cups flour
1 ½ tsps. baking powder
1 tsp. baking soda
2 cups oatmeal
1 cup coconut
2 cups Rice Krispies

Sift together flour, baking powder and baking soda. Mix together the margarine, sugars, eggs and vanilla. Add flour mixture; then add remaining ingredients. Mix well. Drop spoonful on greased cookie sheet and bake at 350 degrees F for 10 to 12 minutes.

Peanut Butter Cookies

½ cup margarine
½ cup brown sugar
½ cup white sugar
½ cup peanut butter
1 egg
1 ½ cups flour
¼ tsp. baking soda
¼ tsp. salt
1 tsp. vanilla

Cream margarine, sugars and peanut butter together. Add egg; blend in flour, baking soda, salt and vanilla. Stir well. Shape dough into 1" balls. Arrange in rows on greased cookie sheet. Press each ball with a fork, flattening, making a crisscross design. Bake at 350 degrees F for 10 to 12 minutes, until golden.

Jumbo Raisin Cookies

2 cups raisins
1 cup water
1 cup shortening
2 cups white sugar
3 eggs
1 tsp. vanilla
3 ½ to 4 cups flour
1 tsp. baking powder
1 tsp. baking soda
1 tsp. salt
1 ½ tsps. cinnamon
½ tsp. nutmeg
½ tsp. allspice

Bring water to boil; add raisins and boil for 5 minutes. Let cool. Cream shortening, sugar, eggs and vanilla. Add dry ingredients then add cooled raisins. Stir until well mixed. Drop by teaspoonful onto a greased cookie sheet and bake at 350 degrees F for approximately 12 minutes.

Butter Buds

1 cup shortening - soft
2 cups brown sugar
2 eggs
2 ½ cups flour
1 tsp. baking powder
1 tsp. vanilla
½ cup nuts and raisins – optional
Cinnamon sugar

Cream shortening and sugar together until creamy, add eggs and vanilla stirring until well mixed. Add nuts or raisins, flour and baking powder, mix to a stiff batter. Roll in balls and place on a cookie sheet. Press each ball with a fork, sprinkle with cinnamon mixed with sugar if desired. Bake at 350 degrees F for 12 minutes.

Ha' Pennies

½ cup margarine
1 cup flour
8 ozs. cheddar cheese – grated
3 tbsps. onion soup mix

Mix all the ingredients together and knead to ensure mixture is well mixed. Roll into a log form, wrap in wax paper and refrigerate to set for 1 hour. Preheat oven to 350 degrees F. Slice dough 1" thick, place on greased cookie sheet and bake for 10 to 12 minutes.
Makes 3 dozen

Mincemeat Hermits

1 ½ cups sugar
2 eggs-well beaten
1 tsp. salt
1 level tsp. soda dissolved in ½ cup sour milk
½ tsp. cloves
1 cup mincemeat
½ cup butter
1 tsp. cinnamon
½ tsp. nutmeg
3 cups flour

Cream butter, add sugar, eggs, salt and sour milk with soda. Sift flour with spices and add, then add mincemeat. Chill, drop by teaspoon on greased cookie sheet and bake at 325 degrees F until golden.

Mrs. Ed (Margaret) Hegedus -dad's cousin

Dad's Cookies

1 cup white sugar
½ cup brown sugar
1 cup margarine
1 egg
1 tsp. vanilla
1 tsp. baking powder
1 tsp. baking soda
1 ¼ cups oatmeal
1 ½ cups flour
¼ cup coconut

Cream sugars and margarine together until creamy. Stir in egg. Add oatmeal, flour, baking powder and baking soda. Mix well to a smooth batter. Shape batter into a roll, wrap in wax paper and place in fridge until firm. Once firm, slice about ½" thick, place on a greased cookie sheet and bake at 400 degrees F for 8 to 10 minutes.

Brownies

1/3 cup oil
2 ozs. unsweetened chocolate
2 eggs
¾ cup sugar
½ cup corn syrup
1 tsp. vanilla
¾ cup flour
½ tsp. salt
½ tsp. baking powder
¾ cup chopped walnuts

Preheat oven to 350 degrees F. Grease 8" square pan. Mix together oil and chocolate in sauce pan, cook over low heat until oil and chocolate melts. Cool. Add eggs one at a time beating by hand until smooth, beat after each addition. Beat in by hand the sugar, syrup and vanilla. Sift dry ingredients together. Add to chocolate mixture. Beat till smooth. Add nuts to batter, pour batter into pan. Bake 40 minutes. Cool before cutting. Makes 16 two inch squares.

Hard Meringues

2 egg whites
Pinch salt
½ tsp. cream of tartar
¾ cup white sugar
½ tsp. vanilla

Combine egg whites, salt and cream of tartar and beat at medium speed with electric mixer until mixture doubles in volume. Increase speed of mixer and start adding sugar slowly, takes about 10 minutes. Beat 5 to 10 minutes longer to dissolve every grain of sugar. The mixture should be able to form peeks. Fold in vanilla. Drop meringue by teaspoonful's onto ungreased paper lined cookie sheet. Bake at 250 degrees F for 1 hour. Turn oven off and leave to dry in oven, 1 hour longer.
Makes 3 dozen

Chow Mein Cookies

1 cup butterscotch chips
1 cup chocolate chips
2 cups Chow Mein noodles
1 cup salted peanuts

Melt chips in double boiler, stir in the noodles and peanuts. Quickly drop by teaspoonful on waxed paper and chill.

Rickey Uncle

½ cup butter
1 cup brown sugar
1 tsp. vanilla
1 tsp. baking soda
2 cups rolled oats

Melt butter in sauce pan on low heat, add brown sugar. Stir until mixed. Add remainder ingredients and mix lightly. Press mixture in a greased 8" x 12" glass baking dish. Bake at 375 degrees F for 12 to 15 minutes until golden brown. Cool and cut into squares.

Oriental Treasures

1 2/3 cups flour
1 ½ tsps. baking powder
½ tsp. soda
½ cup brown sugar- packed
½ cup sugar
½ cup shortening
1 egg
3 tbsps. soya sauce
½ tsp. almond flavoring
½ cup slivered almonds
1 tsp. sugar
½ tsp. soya sauce

Sift together flour, baking powder, soda. Cream brown sugar and white sugar with shortening. Add to flour mixture and add egg, 3 tbsps. soya sauce and almond flavoring. Mix thoroughly, shape dough in small balls and dip in a mixture of slivered almonds, 1 tsp. sugar and ½ tsp. soya sauce. Place on ungreased cookie sheet about 2" apart. Bake for 12 to 15 minutes at 350 degrees F.

****

I remember the Saturday trips to town to grocery shop, and of course, a visit to the Chinese Restaurant on Main Street in Grimshaw. The owner, Dan Suo, would always bring out the cookie container and offer my sisters, brothers and myself, cookies. These cookies were delicious, and had a particular flavor which no other cookie had. They were my favorite.

It has taken me years, of searching to find a recipe which tastes similar to my childhood memory of that particular cookie. I have found this recipe 'Oriental Treasures', which is very similar. A wonderful cookie!

Breakfast Oatmeal Muffins

1 cup flour
1 cup brown sugar
1 tsp. baking powder
1 tsp. baking soda
½ cup oil
2 eggs – beaten
1 cup leftover cooked oatmeal
1 cup raisins
1 tsp. vanilla

Mix ingredients together and stir until batter is well mixed. Grease muffin tin and fill 2/3 full with batter. Bake at 350 degrees F for about 18 minutes or until done.
Yields one dozen

Plain Muffins

1 ¾ cups flour
2 tbsps. sugar
2 ½ tsps. baking powder
¾ tsp. salt
1 egg
¾ cup milk
1/3 cup oil

Mix ingredients together until well mixed. Fill greased muffin tins 2/3 full. Bake for 25 minutes at 400 degrees F.

Morning Glory Muffins

2 cups flour
1 ¼ cups sugar
2 tsps. baking soda
2 tsps. cinnamon
¼ tsp. salt
2 cups shredded carrots
½ cup raisins
½ cup chopped walnuts
½ cup unsweetened flaked coconut
1 apple – peeled, cored and shredded
3 eggs
1 cup vegetable oil
2 tsps. vanilla

Preheat oven to 350 degrees F. Grease 12 muffin cups or line with paper muffin liners. In a large bowl, mix together flour, sugar, baking soda, cinnamon, and salt. Stir in the carrots, raisins, nuts, coconut and apple. In a separate bowl, beat together eggs, oil and vanilla. Stir egg mixture into the carrot/flour mixture, just until moistened. Scoop batter into prepared muffin cups. Bake in preheated oven for 20 minutes, until a toothpick inserted into center of a muffin comes out clean.
Yields 12 muffins

Tasty breakfast muffin for those on the go.

Corn Meal Muffins

½ cup corn meal
1 cup flour
3 tsps. baking powder
1 tbsp. sugar
1/2 tsp. salt
1 tbsp. melted margarine
¾ cup milk
1 egg

Mix dry ingredients. Gradually add milk and egg. Beat well and then add melted margarine, stir thoroughly. Bake in muffin pans in hot oven at 400 degrees F about 25 minutes. Serve muffins warm.

Popovers

2 eggs
1 cup milk
1 cup flour
½ tsp. salt
1 tbsp. oil

Beat together ingredients for 1½ minutes except oil. Add oil, and beat ½ minute more. Pour batter into custard cups filling half full, bake 15 minutes at 475 degrees F. Reduce heat to 350 degrees F and bake for another 25 to 30 minutes. Before removing popovers from oven, prick each one. To dry, turn oven off and leave popovers in oven for 30 minutes with oven door half open. Fill center of popovers with whipped cream.

DESSERTS

Rice Pudding
Baked in Oven

1 to 1 ½ cups rice- cooked
1 cup raisins – optional
1 tsp. cinnamon
½ tsp. nutmeg
2 eggs
2 cups milk
½ cup brown sugar

Beat eggs and milk together. Add remaining ingredients and mix well. Pour into a greased one quart casserole. Set casserole in a pan of 2" deep water. Bake 325 degrees F for 1 hour until set.
Yields 4 – 6 servings

Rice Pudding
Baked in Micro-Wave

1 to 1 ½ cups rice- cooked
1 cup raisins – optional
1 tsp. cinnamon
½ tsp. nutmeg
2 eggs
2 cups milk
½ cup brown sugar

Beat eggs and milk together, add remaining ingredients and mix well. Pour into a greased one quart casserole. Sprinkle cinnamon to top, cover with lid. Cook for 25 minutes on high until set.
Yields 4 to 6 servings.

Rice Pudding

2 eggs
½ cup sugar
½ tsp. salt
2 ¼ cups milk
1 tsp. vanilla
2 cups steamed rice
Dash of cinnamon

Separate eggs. Beat yolks. Add sugar, salt, milk, vanilla and rice to egg yolks and stir. Beat egg whites and fold into mixture. Turn into baking dish. Sprinkle with cinnamon. Bake in oven at 350 degrees F for 45 minutes. Serve hot.

Bread Pudding
Micro-Wave

6 slices bread
2 ½ cups milk
2 eggs- beaten
½ cup raisins – optional
2 apples – peeled and chopped – optional
½ brown sugar
1 tsp. vanilla
½ tsp. cinnamon

Cut bread into ½ inch cubes and set aside. Grease baking dish. In a bowl, mix beaten eggs, sugar, milk, vanilla together whipping till frothy. Place bread cubes into a greased baking dish. Pour liquid mixture over the bread cubes until covered. Fold in apples and raisins into mixture. Sprinkle with cinnamon. Cover baking dish and bake in micro-wave for 20 minutes.

Bread Pudding

6 slices of bread
8 to 12 eggs
1 ½ cups milk
1 ½ cups sugar
1 tsp. vanilla
½ tsp. cinnamon
¼ tsp. nutmeg

Cut bread into cubes and place into a greased baking dish. Beat eggs until foamy and then add milk, sugar, vanilla, cinnamon and nutmeg, mixing well. Pour over bread cubes and let mixture soak into and covering bread cubes. Cover with lid and bake in oven at 375 degrees F for 1 ½ hours.

Fresh Fruit Bread Pudding

12 slices of one or two day old bread- cut in cubes
2 tbsps. butter or margarine
8 eggs
¾ cup brown sugar
1 tsp. cinnamon
½ tsp. allspice – optional
½ tsp. salt
1 tsp. vanilla
4 cups milk
½ cup raisins – optional
2 apples or/and 2 pears or/and any fresh fruit – chopped – optional

Lightly grease casserole dish with butter or margarine. Layer dish with ½ fruit combination, cover with layers of bread cubes, do a second layer ending with bread cubes. In large bowl mix eggs, milk, brown sugar, cinnamon, allspice, salt and vanilla. Beat and pour over layers of bread, pressing bread down to make sure all is soaked. Prepare oven at 350 degrees F, bake in oven for 1 ½ hours.

From my dear friend Bernadette Harris
January 31, 1994

Milk Pudding
Micro-Waved

In large glass bowl scald 2 cups milk in micro-wave, about 3 minutes.

Mix together-
1 egg- beaten
2 tbsps. corn starch
1 tbsp. flour
¼ tsp. salt
½ cup sugar or ¾ cup brown sugar
1 tsp. vanilla – prefer pure vanilla
½ cup milk

Add ingredients to scalded milk and stir until well blended. Micro-wave on high for 2 minutes, stirring every minute until mixture thickens and comes to a boil. Stir in 1 tbsp. margarine. Ready to serve.

Tapioca Pudding
Micro-Waved

3 tbsps. tapioca
3 eggs
1 tsp. vanilla flavoring
4 cups milk
1 cup white sugar
3 tbsps. sugar

Soak the tapioca in warm water for 2 hours. Drain off water and pour tapioca into the scalded milk, let boil for 15 minutes, stirring constantly. In separate bowl beat together the yolks of eggs and sugar, then stir into the pudding mix and add vanilla. Pour into a baking dish. Cook on high for 20 minutes. Beat egg whites with 3 tbsps. sugar with an egg beater until stiff and frothy. Fold into pudding and bake on high another 5 minutes.

Baked Custard

3 eggs
½ cup sugar
¼ tsp. salt
1 tsp. vanilla
2 cups scalded milk
½ tsp. nutmeg or cinnamon

Beat eggs slightly with a fork. Stir in sugar, salt and vanilla. Add a little of the hot milk to the egg mixture and stir; add remaining milk and mix well. Pour into a baking dish, sprinkle with nutmeg or cinnamon. Bake at 350 degrees F for 50 to 60 minutes or until firm. To test- poke a sharp knife into center, if knife comes out clean, then custard is done.
8 servings

Blanc Mange

1/3 cup sugar
¼ cup cornstarch
¼ tsp. salt
2 cups scalded milk, cooled
½ tsp. vanilla

In the top of a double boiler, combine sugar, cornstarch and salt, mix thoroughly. Place top on bottom of double boiler over lightly boiling water. Gradually add milk, stirring constantly until mixture thickens. Remove from heat and stir in vanilla. Pour into serving dishes. Serve warm or cold, plain or with a sauce. 6 servings

Apple-Oatmeal Crisp Pudding

3 or 4 cooking apples
½ cup margarine
¾ cup quick-cooking oatmeal
1 tsp. cinnamon
¼ cup white sugar
¾ cup brown sugar – packed
½ cup flour

Pare apples, slice thinly. Arrange in buttered baking dish. Sprinkle with white sugar. Be sure sugar covers all of the apples. In bowl mix flour, cinnamon, brown sugar and oatmeal. Stir and add margarine, cut in to a crumbly mix.. Sprinkle mix over apples. Bake in oven at 350 degrees F for 25 minutes until crumbs are golden and apples are soft when pierced with fork.
*or Microwave for 16 to 20 minutes on high or until apples are tender

****

My family's favorite.

Yogurt & Granola

1 cup yogurt – plain or any flavor
1 cup fresh berries – any of your favorite
¼ cup granola

Layer berries then yogurt in a glass cup and sprinkle on top with granola.
*use a small glass dish or fancy glass cup to make the serving look special.

Fresh Fruit Desserts

Saskatoon's, Raspberries, Strawberries (Wild or Tame)

Wash fresh picked berries in cold water, drain and serve with fresh cream and sprinkle with sugar or whipping cream or ice cream.

Apple Bake

1 apple - per serving
1 tsp. brown sugar

Carve a hole at the top of the apple, remove the core and seeds. Fill the top of the apple with brown sugar. Place apple in a baking dish with about 1" of water. Bake in oven at 350 degrees F until apple is done.

****

Baked apples were one of the desserts my mother cooked in the oven of the old wood stove on the farm, when I was a young girl.

Apple Bake with Cinnamon

1 apple per serving
¼ tsp. cinnamon

Peel and slice apple, removing the core and seeds. Place apple slices on a plate, sprinkle with cinnamon and bake in the micro-wave for about 1 to 2 minutes or until tender.

An easy and quick treat.

****

Days long gone, I remember when company came for a visit. These visits could last all afternoon or all evening. Mom would make tea and set the table with sandwiches and baked goods. Even if there were no baked goods, sandwiches were always served. No one left without good conversation, and a full stomach.

FUDGE – CANDY – FROSTINGS

That Old Favorite – Fudge

2 cups sugar
2 ozs. of chocolate
¾ cup milk
¼ cup margarine
½ tsp. salt
1 tsp. vanilla extract
½ cup chopped walnuts

Combine chocolate, milk, sugar, margarine, salt in medium sauce pan. Bring to a boil, stirring constantly. Continue to boil to 240 degrees F until a small amount of mixture forms soft ball when tested in cold water. Cool to lukewarm and add vanilla and nuts. Beat in saucepan until it holds its shape, about 1 to 3 minutes. Immediately pour into a greased pan. Cool and cut into 30 pieces.

Divinity Fudge

2 ½ cups sugar
½ cup syrup
½ cup hot water
2 egg whites – stiffly beaten
1 tsp. vanilla
Few drops of almond extract
½ cup walnuts – chopped

Boil sugar, syrup and water to 240 degrees F or until mixture forms a soft ball when tested in cold water. Beat continually, pour half of hot syrup mixture over beaten egg whites, and blend well. Return remaining syrup to heat and boil to hard ball stage. Slowly pour over egg mixture. Beat well and when thickened add flavoring and nuts. Pour into greased pan to harden.

Maple Sugar Fudge

2 cups brown sugar
¾ cup milk
¼ cup margarine
½ tsp. salt
1 tsp. maple extract
½ cup chopped walnuts -optional

Combine milk, brown sugar, margarine, and salt in medium sauce pan. Bring to a boil, stirring constantly. Continue to boil to 240 degrees F until a small amount of mixture forms soft ball when tested in cold water. Cool to lukewarm and add maple extract and nuts. Beat in saucepan until it holds its shape. About 1 to 3 minutes. Immediately pour into a greased pan. Makes 30 pieces.

Toffee

1 – 14 oz. can sweeten condensed milk
2 cups brown sugar
½ cup corn syrup
6 tbsps. oil
1/8 tsp. salt

Mix all ingredients in a sauce pan; bring to a boil, stirring constantly. Continue to cook over low heat and stir until mixture forms a hard ball when tested in cold water, or has reached the hard ball stage on a candy thermometer. Remove from heat, stir for about 3 minutes until thick and sticky, pour into buttered pan. Cool and cut in pieces.
*testing without a candy thermometer by dipping a ½ tsp. of mixture in ice cold water to check to see if it forms a hard ball.

Popcorn Caramel Crunch

4 cups popped popcorn
1 cup dry roasted peanuts
1 cup chow mein noodles
½ cup raisins
1 cup sugar
¾ cup butter
½ cup light corn syrup
2 tbsps. water
1 tsp. ground cinnamon

In a large greased bowl, combine the first four ingredients; set aside. In a large saucepan, combine sugar, butter, corn syrup and water. Cook over medium heat, stirring occasionally, until a candy thermometer reads 280 degrees F to 290 degrees F (soft crack stage) Remove from heat; stir in cinnamon. Pour over popcorn mixture and stir until evenly coated. Immediately pour popcorn mixture onto a greased cookie sheet. When cool enough to handle, break into pieces. Store in an airtight container.
Makes about 8 cups.

Popcorn Balls

10 cups popped popcorn
1 cup sugar
½ cup water
¼ cup light corn syrup
½ tsp. vinegar
½ tsp. vanilla

Measure popcorn in buttered bowl. Combine in a sauce pan, sugar, water, corn syrup and vinegar. Stir over heat until sugar is dissolved. Cover, bring to boil and let boil briskly for about 3 minutes. Uncover, liquid should be at hard ball stage. Remove from heat, stir in vanilla. Pour slowly over popcorn. Stir until popcorn is covered. Rub margarine on your hands, and then start forming balls about 2 ½" in diameter.
Makes 12 popcorn balls.

Maple Icing

2 cups icing sugar
2 tbsps. margarine
Milk
½ tsp. maple extract

Blend icing sugar and margarine together until smooth, stir in enough milk to make a thick paste or medium frosting. Add maple flavoring and mix well. Make a thickness that is easy to spread.

Maple Icing

2 tbsps. soft margarine
1 cup brown sugar
1 tbsp. maple syrup

Mix together, if icing is too soft add a bit more sugar, if too stiff a bit more syrup.

Aunt Eva's Maple Icing

1 cup brown sugar
¼ cup flour
1 tsp. maple flavoring
Water

Mix brown sugar and flour together, adding enough water to make a paste, add flavoring. Stir ingredients until the mixture is thick and smooth, ready to spread on cake.

****

I first tasted maple icing at my Great Aunt Eva's in Wakaw, Sask. when my family went for a summer visit in 1964. It was an interesting recipe, and I thought it an unusual mixture for an icing. However, it was tasty. No one would know that this icing had flour in it. From time to time, I use this icing for my own cakes.

Shannon's Wedding Cake Icing

8 oz. cream cheese – room temperature
½ cup butter or margarine
1 tbsp. lemon juice
Icing sugar – enough to make a thick paste

Add first three ingredients together and melt over low heat, stirring until well mixed. Add icing sugar gradually and mix until desired thickness. Will cover a 9" x 13" cake.

Seven-Minute Frosting

1 cup white sugar
1/8 tsp. cream of tartar
Pinch of salt
1 egg white – unbeaten
1/3 cup boiling water
½ tsp. vanilla

Mix all ingredients together (except vanilla) in top of double boiler; stir to dissolve sugar. Set pan over boiling water and beat with electric beater until stiff enough to stand in peaks. Remove from heat; add vanilla and continue to beating until stiff enough to spread. Use immediately. Yields enough for a large layer cake.

Old Fashioned Brown Sugar Syrup

1 ½ cups brown sugar
½ tsp. vanilla
¼ tsp. cinnamon – optional
¾ cup water

Combine sugar and water, stir until dissolved. Boil 2 to 3 minutes, until syrup is a thickness you prefer. Add flavoring and stir until well mixed. Serve hot or cold. Can store in covered jar in the refrigerator.
Makes 1 cup
*other flavors can be used - maple
*can be served on pancakes, waffles or French toast

Spud Nut Glaze

1 ½ cups milk
1 ½ cup sugar

Stir together and bring to a boil, stirring constantly. Turn heat to low, keeping the glaze simmering. Dip each doughnut in glaze. If the glaze thickens, add a little milk.

Almond Paste

3 cups white sugar
1 ½ cups hot water
2 tsps. cream of tarter
3 cups almond nuts – finely chopped –optional
Almond extract – few drops
2 egg yolks

Boil sugar, water and cream of tartar together, stirring until mixture forms a soft ball. (when a small portion is tested when dipped in cold water). Stir in yolks and almond extract. Stir until a stiff paste is formed and ready for spreading.
*use on Great Grandma Ireland's spice cake

Philadelphia Cream Cheese Icing

1 – 8 oz. pkg. Philadelphia cream cheese
¼ cup margarine
1 tsp. vanilla
3 cups powdered sugar

Beat cream cheese, margarine and vanilla together in a large bowl with an electric mixer on medium speed. Add sugar gradually, beating until well blended. Make enough icing for a 9" x 9" cake.

Glaze for Doughnuts

½ cup margarine
1 cup sugar
¼ cup milk
1 cup icing sugar
½ tsp. salt
½ tsp. vanilla

Boil margarine, sugar and milk for exactly one minute; then add remaining ingredients. Stir. Cool and spoon over doughnuts.

BEVERAGES – PUNCHES – SHAKES

Beverages

Afternoon Tea-

I remember when this delightful form of entertainment was practiced everywhere; however today, it is not so common. Little preparation was needed, and it came at the most leisurely hour of the day, three o'clock. Tea time gave the family a chance to chat with each other or with friends.

This was a traditional event in my family while growing up, and my parents continued it throughout their lives. At three o'clock, I always knew tea would be on at mom and dad's house, no matter what day it was.

Tea time was an event in itself. RED ROSE tea had to be steeped just right or it was not a good cup of tea. I am sure my parents were the connoisseurs of teas, especially mom. She never liked drinking tea at the restaurant. She said it was not hot enough nor was it steeped properly.

Morning Coffee-

As a youngster, I remember waking up in the early mornings, smelling the aroma of NABOB coffee filtering through the air into my bedroom, which I shared with four sisters. Every day, dad would have the old coffee pot on the wood cook stove brewing to perfection. In my teenage years, I was told coffee would stunt my growth, if I drank coffee. Not likely, I am five feet five inches, so drinking coffee didn't affect me in any way.

Today, enjoying a good cup of coffee or two in the morning is a ritual in my life. Coffee starts the day off, as it must have been for my parents. Sitting holding a warm cup, smelling the flavor brings back many memories and planning of the day.

As times have passed, the event of making coffee or even drinking coffee has changed. I have gone from learning how to brew a decent pot of coffee on a wood cook stove, to a natural gas stove, to an electric coffee pot, then to a drip coffee maker, and now to a push button machine, which makes one cup at a time, any flavor you desire. How times have changed!

Wild Mint

Wild Mint -Mentha arvensis
Although mint had long been used for different purposes, Native Americans used it for medicinal preparations and as a savory for dried meats. The native mint (Mentha arvensis), not to be confused with the peppermint or spearmint, was well known to the Plains Indians. It is a familiar, common plant, looks like a true mint, and its pungent, aromatic scent cannot be mistaken. The dried leaves and flowering tops were used in the same way as other mints; in aromatic stimulant beverages, and to relieve nausea, gas, and pain in the stomach and bowels. All of the great Canadian tribes used the various mints for these and related ills.

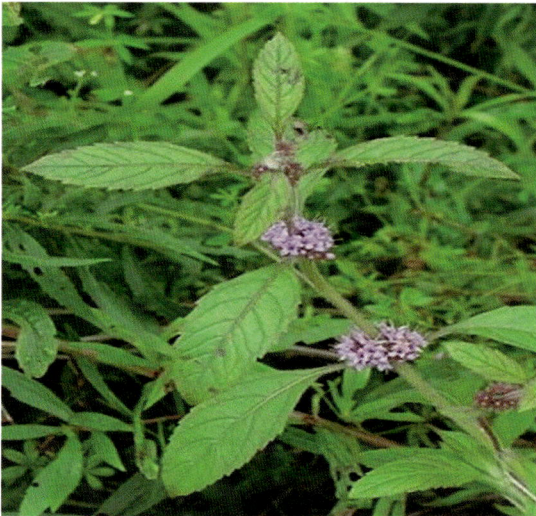

Wild mint is harvested at a certain time of the year. When the plant reached 8 inches tall, and should be cut back at no more than six inches. Two inches of plant should always be left to avoid killing the mint plant. Mint can be harvested several times throughout the spring, summer and fall. Dried or fresh mint leaves make excellent tea and is an easy process to learn.

Just follow these steps!

Fill kettle with water and bring it to a boil
While it's boiling, stuff a bunch of leaves loosely into a tall glass or tea pot.
Ruffle the leaves a little- this will encourage the aroma.
Pour the boiling water onto the leaves.
Use sugar or honey to sweeten to taste if needed
It's OK to drink the tea without removing the leaves.

Drying Mint after the Harvest-
Wash the mint and hang it upside down in a dark place where the air can circulate easily around the mint. You can also lay mint flat to dry at room temperature or in a dehydrator. The ideal temperature for drying mint is 85 to 95 degrees F. Dried mint is an excellent herbal tea, and can also be added to soups, stews or jellies. Dried mint also makes an excellent addition to potpourris and crafts.

Freezing Mint After Harvesting-
You can also freeze the mint inside ice cubes to add flavor to drinks, or in butters or oils for cooking.

****

While working in Northern Alberta's Aboriginal communities, I had an opportunity to learn about, and experience the harvesting of wild mint near the community of High Level, Alberta. And I also learned how to make a fresh cup of wild mint tea, which I enjoyed.

With my new knowledge I told mom about my teachings. She informed me that as children, they would go with their mother, Gladys Andrews, and harvest wild mint in the valley near the Smoky along the Peace.

This was a yearly undertaking, and they would amble through the bush and wetlands until they found a good growing crop of wild mint to harvest.
My grandmother harvested wild mint not only for making tea but to dry into fine flakes as flavoring for the icing or topping of cakes, desserts, or as a sweetener. She also used it for settling upset stomachs.

Sharing this bit of history is important because it demonstrates what herbs the pioneers learned to use from Mother Nature, and was another way of living off the land.

Old English Eggnog

6 egg yolks
1 cup sugar
8 cups light cream
2 cups cognac
1 cup light rum
6 egg whites
½ cup sugar

In a large bowl, beat egg yolks until thick. Gradually add sugar beating until light. Add cream, beat until well mixed. Slowly pour in cognac and rum. Place in refrigerator until chilled. One hour before serving beat egg whites until foamy. Add sugar, continue to beat until foamy stiff peak form. Fold mixture into egg yolk mixture. Refrigerate until ready to serve.
Makes 28 – 4 oz. servings

A Christmas drink of Cheers!

Trader's Punch

2 cups orange juice
2 cups lemon juice
2 cups grenadine syrup
10 cups ginger ale
Crushed ice
1 lemon
6 cherries

Mix liquids together in a glass punch bowl. Stir and add 2 cups crushed ice. Decorate punch by slicing lemon thin and place slices on top of punch, place a ½ cherry on top of lemon slice.
Makes 4 quarts (16 cups)

****

I had the pleasure of making Trader's Punch for my sister Terean's wedding, and for my niece Penny's wedding. This is a great non-alcohol punch suitable for any occasion.

Jolly Holly Punch

2/3 cup unsweetened pineapple
6 ozs. lemonade – concentrated
¼ cup lime juice
1 ½ cups club soda
1 – 48 oz. Hawaiian punch
2 cups crushed ice

Pour all the ingredients together into a punch bowl.
Ready to be served.

After-School Strawberry Shake

2 cups strawberries - stemmed
2 medium bananas - peeled and cut into 1" pieces
3 cups ice cubes - divided
½ cup non-fat strawberry or plain yogurt
½ cup orange juice – optional
2 tbsps. honey
*can use pineapple juice in place of orange juice

Place all ingredients except 1 ½ cups of the ice cubes in a blender; blend on high speed until smooth, scraping sides down of blender occasionally. Add remaining ice; continue to blend until smooth.
Serve in tall glasses; dividing equally
Makes 3 servings.

Watermelon Strawberry Shake

1-8oz. container lemon non-fat yogurt
2 cups watermelon - cubed and seeded
2 cups fresh strawberries - cleaned and hulled
1 medium banana - peeled and sliced

In a blender or food processor mix yogurt, watermelon, strawberries and banana until smooth and frothy. Makes 4 servings.

SOUPS

Dianne's Cabbage Soup

1 large onion - diced
2 cans green cut beans - optional
2 large cans of stewed seasoned tomatoes
1 medium head of cabbage - chopped
6 sticks of celery - chopped
1 pkg. onion soup mix or chicken noodle mix
½ lb. of carrots - chopped
1 large can of beef or chicken broth
Season with salt, pepper, onion salt, parsley flakes.
10 cups water

Cut onions, cabbage, carrots and celery into small pieces and add to boiling water. Stir and add remaining ingredients and seasonings. Cook for about 15 minutes then reduce heat to simmer and continue cooking till veggies are tender. May add more seasoning for taste. Makes a large pot.

Tomato Macaroni Soup

2 cups water
1 can tomato soup
¼ cup onions - chopped fine
¼ cup celery - chopped fine
Salt, pepper, celery salt, onion salt to season for taste
1/8 cup macaroni - elbow or shell (small)

Fill sauce pan with water and bring to a boil, add onion and celery. Cook until tender; add tomato soup. Stir and add seasonings to taste. Add macaroni, stir well, and continue to cook on medium heat for about ½ hour or until macaroni is well cooked. Add more seasoning if required.

Turkey Noodle Soup

6 cups water
Turkey bones with meat on (roasted turkey left over's)
2 cubes of chicken bouillon
1 cup cooked turkey - cubes
1 medium onion - diced
3 sticks celery - diced
4 carrots - diced
2 large potatoes - diced
Salt
Pepper
Onion salt or powder or dried flakes
Celery salt
Parsley flakes
1 ½ cups egg noodles

Fill large pot with water and bring to a boil. Add cooked turkey bones and cook until meat falls off the bones. Remove bones, stir and add chicken bouillon and seasonings to taste. Add cubed cooked turkey, onion, celery, carrots and potatoes and continue to cook until vegetables are tender; stir in noodles and continue to cook on medium heat for about ½ hour or until noodles are soft. Add more seasoning if required.

Vegetable Soup

2 cups water
1 can tomato soup
1 can vegetable broth or beef broth
1 small onion - diced
2 sticks celery - diced
4 carrots - diced
1 large potato - diced
Salt
Pepper
Onion salt or powder or dried flakes
Celery salt
Parsley flakes

Fill sauce pan with water and bring to a boil, add vegetables, cook until tender; add tomato soup and broth. Stir and add seasonings to taste. Cook on medium heat for about ½ hour. Add more seasoning if require

Ham and Bean Soup

2 cups water
1 can tomato soup
1 can pork n beans
½ onion - chopped
3 sticks celery - chopped
Salt
Pepper
1 cup cooked ham - cubes

Fill medium sauce pan half full of water and bring to a boil, add onion and celery, cook until tender; add soup, pork & beans, pepper, salt and ham. Stir well, and continue to cook on medium heat for about ½ hour. Add more seasoning if required.
Can add dumplings if desired.
SOUP IS READY!
See Dumpling recipe-

117

Bean and Wiener Soup

2 cups water
1 can tomato soup
1 can pork & beans
½ onion - chopped
3 sticks celery- chopped
Salt
Pepper
4 wieners – cut up in chunks
1/8 cup macaroni – optional

Fill medium sauce pan half full of water and bring to a boil, add onion and celery, cook until tender; add soup, pork & beans, pepper, salt, wieners and macaroni. Stir well, and continue to cook on medium heat for about ½ hour or until macaroni is soft. Add more seasoning if required.

A quick and easy soup for anytime!

Onion Soup

2 tbsps. margarine
4 medium onions
4 cups beef stock or bouillon cubes
1 tsp. salt
1/8 tsp. black pepper
½ tsp. Worcestershire sauce
6 slices of bread – French
Parmesan cheese – grated

Melt margarine in frying pan. Slice onions diagonally, add to melted margarine, and cook gently until lightly browned, stir frequently. Stir in beef stock, salt, pepper and Worcestershire sauce. Cover and simmer on medium heat for 30 minutes. Taste for seasoning. Pour onion soup into bowls and grate cheese over soup and serve hot. Serve with toasted sliced bread. Recipe can be frozen. Serves 6

Beef Stew

5 cups water
1 lb. beef or moose – cut into cubes
2 tbsps. olive oil
2 large onions – diced
4 cups carrots – sliced
2 large potatoes – cut into cubes
2 cups turnips – cut into cubes
4 sticks of celery – sliced – optional
Salt
Pepper
2 cubes of beef oxo

In a large non-stick pot, add oil and heat over medium high heat. Add beef or moose chunks; sauté until browned. Add onions continue to sauté, stirring continuously until done. Add salt, pepper and beef oxo. Add enough water to cover the meat and onions. Bring to a boil then reduce heat to simmer until the meat is cooked and tender. May need to add more water and continue to simmer. Add carrots, potatoes, celery, turnips and cover to continue to simmer until vegetables are tender. Simmer for about 1 hour.
*if the liquid is not covering the meat and vegetables add more.

Add dumplings if desired.

SANDWICHES

Meat Spreads

A delicious variety of ways to serve a sandwich or bun which looks and tastes great!

Spread-
1 cup meat - chopped finely – (wieners, canned meats or cooked meats)
¼ cup onion - chopped finely or ¼ cup dill pickles - chopped
¼ cup miracle whip

Mix all ingredients together until well mixed. Spread on bread or toast or halves of buns or crackers

Quick and easy, ready to serve for lunch!

Salmon or Tuna Spreads

Spread-
1 can salmon or tuna
¼ cup onion - Spanish or green onion chopped finely
¼ cup Miracle Whip
Salt and pepper - season to taste

Mix all ingredients together until well mixed.
Spread on bread – various kinds or halves of buns or crackers

Quick and easy spread ready to serve for lunch or afternoon tea!

Egg Salad Spread

Spread-
2 eggs – boiled
Salt and pepper to season
2 tbsps. Miracle Whip
1 green onion – chopped

Mix all ingredients together until well mixed. Ready to spread on a bun or toast.

Open Face Bun

1 bun – sliced in half
Egg or meat spread
Lettuce – enough to cover bun
1 tsp. margarine
Salt and pepper to season
Paprika – optional

Using any type of bun, plain or toasted, spread margarine on, add lettuce, and then add egg or meat spread. Sprinkle with paprika, ready to serve. Serving for one.

Pizza Bun

Make your own pizza bun!

Spread-
1 – 7 ½ oz. can tomato sauce or tomato soup
¼ tsp. oregano
1 small onion- grated -optional
½ tsp. garlic salt- optional
½ tsp. lemon pepper-optional
½ lb. cheddar cheese – medium or mozzarella – grated

Combine ingredients together except cheese. Spread generously on plain or onion bun halves.
Top with any of the following combinations or your favorites.

Olives – sliced
Salami, pepperoni, ham, bologna – sliced
Mushrooms – sliced
Green Peppers – sliced

Sprinkle over topping with cheese. Place in an oven and broil until top bubbles. Serves 6

****
Easy for the teenagers to make, and for the family to enjoy.

Toasted Bacon /Tomato/Cheese/Lettuce/ Sandwich

2 bread slices
1 cheese slice
3 bacon strips – cooked (pork or turkey)
½ tomato- sliced
Lettuce – enough to cover slice of bread
1 tsp. margarine
1 tbsp. miracle whip

Toast bread using any type of breads, spread margarine and miracle whip on toasted bread, add slice of cheese, tomato, lettuce and then add 3 strips cooked bacon. Cover with second slice of toasted bread. Slice in half and ready to serve. Serving for one.

KETCHUP PLEASE!

Any Kind of Meat & Cheese Sandwich

2 bread slices
1 cheese slice
1 meat slice – cooked or sliced meat
1 tsp. margarine
1 tsp. mustard

Plain or toasted bread using any type of bread, spread margarine and mustard on bread, add slice of cheese and then meat. Slice in half and ready to serve. Serving for one.

Grilled Cheese Sandwich

2 bread slices
1 cheddar cheese slice
1 tsp. margarine
1 tbsp. oil
Meat slices- optional

Take two slices of bread, place sliced cheese in between bread, and spread margarine on outside of sandwich. Prepare by heating skillet on medium heat, add oil then set sandwich into the skillet. Once one side is golden brown, turn over and brown the other side.
Ready to serve hot.

Open Face Cheese

1 slice of bread
Cheese - hard or cheese slice
1 tbsp. margarine
1 slice of onion – optional
1 slice of bologna - optional

Toast bread, spread margarine onto bread and place onion and/or bologna and sliced hard cheese on top. Place toast into broiler oven and cook until cheese is melted. Serving for one.

Old Cheddar & Syrup Sandwich

2 slices of bread
3 slices of old cheddar cheese
1 tsp. margarine
1 tbsp. Rodgers Syrup

Spread margarine onto bread, place sliced cheese on top, then spread on syrup. Cover with second slice of bread. Cut in half and ready to eat. Serving for one.

****

Old Cheddar and Syrup sandwiches were a childhood sandwich, we would often have for snacks, and even in our school lunches. We thought we were quite lucky with our cheese and syrup sandwiches, instead of the good old peanut butter and jam sandwiches. Some school kids were less fortunate as their sandwiches were not very interesting. However I never paid much attention to what other kids ate. I was too busy getting lunch time over with, so I could go outdoors and spend time on the swings.

Toasted Fried Egg & Cheese Sandwich

2 bread slices-any type
1 cheddar cheese slice
1 egg – fried
1 tsp. margarine
1 tbsp. oil
Salt and pepper to season

Toast bread, spread margarine on toasted bread, add slice of cheese and fried egg. Add salt and pepper to season. Slice in half and ready to serve. Serving for one.

Ham /Cheese/Egg Sandwich

2 bread slices-any type
1 cheese slice
1 ham slice– cooked
1 egg
1 tsp. margarine

Toast bread, spread margarine on toasted bread, add slice of ham, cheese and fried egg. Cover with second toast and slice in half, ready to serve. Serving for one.

OH YOU MAY NEED KETCHUP!

Toasted Fried Egg Sandwich

2 bread slices- any type
1 egg - fried hard
1 tsp. margarine
1 tbsp. oil
Salt and pepper to season

Toast bread, spread margarine on toasted bread, and add fried egg, salt and pepper to season. Slice in half and ready to serve.
Serving for one

Onion Sandwich

2 slices of bread
5 onion slices - thinly
1 tsp. margarine
1 tbsp. Miracle Whip
Sprinkle of salt – optional

Bread may be plain or toasted. Spread margarine and Miracle Whip onto bread, and then add sliced onion on top, cover with second slice of bread. Cut in half and ready to serve. Serving for one.

****

Onion sandwiches may be an acquired taste for some; however they are quite good if your stomach has the constitution. Younger stomachs can handle the onions, but as one gets older the stomach tends to not appreciate such foods, resulting in acid reflux and heart burn. Also, always remember, if you plan to eat an onion sandwich, make sure you are not going out to visit anyone or going to work the next day. Your colleagues may not appreciate you and keep their distance.

Peanut Butter & Banana Open Face Sandwich

1 slice of bread
1 banana – sliced
1 tbsp. peanut butter
½ tsp. margarine

Bread may be plain or toasted. Spread margarine and peanut butter onto bread, then place sliced banana on top. Ready to eat. Serving for one.

Dill Pickle Sandwich

2 slices of bread
Dill pickles- sliced thinly
1 tsp. margarine

Spread margarine onto bread, then place sliced pickles on top, cover with second slice of bread. Cut in half and ready to serve. Serving for one.

Radish Sandwich

2 slices of bread
Radishes– sliced thinly
1 tsp. margarine
1 tsp. mayonnaise

Spread margarine and mayonnaise onto bread, then place sliced radishes on top, cover with second slice of bread and cut in half and ready to serve. Serving for one.

Lettuce Leaf Roll

1 large lettuce leaf
Sugar

Wash one large lettuce leaf, sprinkle with sugar, fold end in and roll the leaf. Ready to eat.

Cinnamon Toast

1 slice of bread
1 tsp. margarine
Sugar
Cinnamon

Spread margarine on toasted bread, sprinkle sugar then cinnamon onto toast. Serving for one.

Camp Fire Toasted Cheese Sandwich

2 slices of bread
1 slice of cheese or cheese whiz
1 tbsp. margarine
Foil wrap

Place cheese between two slices of bread, spread margarine on the outside of the two sides. Wrap into foil wrap with shiny side inward. Place foiled sandwich on a stick or a barbeque fork and hold over an open fire, turning occasionally until done. Now it's time for a grilled cheese sandwich.

Great on snowmobile outings or when camping!

****

In later years, Stephen told me that one of his best memories was our snowmobiling outings and the grilled cheese sandwiches. We would gather with our friends and their children and go out snowmobiling on sunny wintery Sundays. Our old yellow ski-doo would be hooked up to the caboose, shaped like a missile sitting on skis. Once everyone was dressed in their over- stuffed ski-doo suits and snacks prepared, the family was ready to jump on and in the old yellow machine. We would head east out of town, across the fields to a small ravine. The children would bring their crazy carpets and toboggans and spend their afternoon, sliding down a small hill into a gully. Up and down they went. We would prepare a bonfire, ready for roasting snacks. The kids would toast grilled cheese sandwiches, and of course, wieners. This was a wonderful time spent with family and friends.

SALADS

Broccoli Salad

½ stalk of broccoli – cut into bite size pieces
6 slices turkey bacon- cooked and chopped- optional
1 large apple – diced
½ cup raisins or cranberries
½ cup old cheddar cheese – cubed

In a large bowl, toss together broccoli, bacon, apple, raisins and cheese. Add dressing and mix well. Refrigerate for at least 1 hour before serving. Makes 6 servings.
*can use Ranch dressing

See Creamy Dressing recipe-

Coleslaw Salad

½ head of green cabbage – finely grated
2 carrots – grated
3 tbsps. mayonnaise
Salt & pepper to season to taste

Mix together the cabbage and carrots and add mayonnaise or a coleslaw dressing.

See Coleslaw Dressing recipe-

Caesar Salad

1 head Romaine lettuce
1 tomato- cubed
1 can black olives - sliced
Cheese - grated - optional
Croutons -optional
Caesar dressing

In a bowl, start with Romaine lettuce cut into bite size pieces. Add quartered tomato, black olives and mix in Caesar dressing. Sprinkle grated cheese over top and croutons. Ready to serve.
*do not pour dressing into salad mixture until ready to be serve.

Strawberry Spinach Salad

10 ozs. fresh spinach - cut into bite sizes
½ cup strawberries -sliced
¼ cup almonds - blanched/slivers

In a large bowl combine spinach, strawberries and almonds. Pour dressing over salad, and toss. Refrigerate for 10 to 15 minutes before serving.

See Spinach Dressing recipe-

Spinach with Bacon & Egg Salad

10 ozs. fresh spinach - cut into bite sizes
2 eggs - hard boiled and sliced
¼ cup bacon pieces - cooked and crumbled
1/8 cup of red onion- chopped - optional
Ranch dressing

In a large bowl, place washed, cut spinach. Add onion, sliced boiled eggs and sprinkle bacon pieces on top. Mix lightly. Upon serving add small amount of ranch dressing to taste.

Spinach with Strawberry & Nut Salad

10 ozs. fresh spinach - cut into bite sizes
½ cup strawberries - sliced
½ cup walnuts or almonds- sliced or whole
2 tbsps. margarine
1 tsp. sugar
Raspberry Vinaigrette

In a large bowl, place washed, cut spinach. Add sliced strawberries. In sauce pan melt margarine on low heat, add sugar and walnuts, stir until walnuts are covered with a syrup texture or caramelized. Stir continuously so the walnuts do not burn. Remove from heat and add to salad. Mix lightly. Add small amount of raspberry vinaigrette or dressing of choice before serving.

134

Old Fashion Summer Green Salad

½ head of lettuce - iceberg
1 tomato
½ cucumber
2 green onions
4 radishes – optional
Miracle Whip – use the amount desired
Salt
Pepper

Place in a bowl, lettuce cut into bite size pieces. Add cubed tomato, sliced cucumber and radishes, diced onions and mix in dressing (miracle whip, salt and pepper). Ready to serve.

Chef's Salad

½ head of lettuce - iceberg
1 tomato - cubed
½ cucumbers- sliced
1 stick of celery- chopped
1 green onion - diced
2 sticks of carrots – thinly sliced
2 slices of cooked ham - diced
¼ cup of cheese - grated
2 slices of cooked (variety) meats - diced
2 eggs - boiled - sliced
Salt
Pepper
Paprika
Ranch or Thousand Island dressing or your favorite

Arrange lettuce, cut into bite size pieces on a dinner plate. Add tomato, carrots, cucumber, onion and celery on top of lettuce. Then place meats and egg slices on top of vegetables. Sprinkle with grated cheese and add seasonings to taste. When serving add a small amount of Ranch or Thousand Island dressing to taste. Ready to serve. Makes 2 servings.

Cucumber Salad

2 cups cucumbers – sliced
1 cup white vinegar

Slice fresh firm cucumbers about 1/4" thick, place in a bowl. Pour vinegar over cucumbers and mix. Place in refrigerator to keep cool until ready to serve.

Creamy Cucumber Salad

2 cups cucumbers - sliced
1 cup creamy dressing

Slice fresh firm cucumbers about 1/4" thick, place in a bowl. Pour creamy dressing over cucumbers and mix. Place in refrigerator to keep cool until ready to serve.

See Creamy Dressing recipe-

.

Broccoli & Cauliflower Salad

1 stalk of broccoli- cut into small pieces
½ head of cauliflower - cut into small pieces
2 sticks of carrots - thinly sliced
1 cup ribbon pasta- cooked
Dash of salt & pepper
Creamy dressing - Ranch or Ranch & Bacon

Cook pasta as per pasta directions, drain and pour cold water over pasta until cooled and not sticking together. Set aside. Prepare vegetables and place in a glass bowl. Add cooked pasta and stir. Add seasoning, dressing and mix well. Place in refrigerator to keep cool until ready to serve.

Japanese Salad

½ cup slivered almonds- sliced
2 tbsps. sesame seeds
½ head medium cabbage- chopped finely
1 pkg. bean sprouts
2 cups mushrooms- stems/pieces
2 cups green onions- chopped
¼ cup sunflower seeds
1 – 3 oz. pkg. oriental noodles
½ pkg. Chow Mein noodles – chopped

Prepare all the ingredients together in a large bowl. Pour Japanese Dressing over the dry ingredients, stir and let stand for 1 to 2 hours. Ready to serve.

See Japanese Dressing recipe-

Potato Salad

6 eggs - hard boiled, cooled and sliced
2 potatoes -cooked, cooled and cubed
2 green onions -diced
½ cup Miracle whip
Pepper
Salt
Paprika

Mix in a bowl, sliced eggs, cut up potatoes, and diced onions. Add miracle whip dressing, salt and pepper. Mix well. Sprinkle with paprika. Cool in refrigerator for half hour and serve.

Great summer salad with barbequed steak or hamburgers!

How Cottage Cheese Was Made the Old Fashion Way!

On the farm, cottage cheese didn't come in a plastic container ready to eat. There was a process to making cottage cheese. Every so often mom would make a batch of cottage cheese, by taking the left over sour milk and heat it on the stove, stirring constantly till the milk became thick and lumpy. These lumps were called curds, and as the milk became thicker more curds were formed. Then the liquid was drained off and curds were rinsed with cold water. Then the curds were placed in a cheese cloth, and tied like a beggar's pack sack and hung on the clothes line to dry. It would take some time, because the liquid whey dripped out of the cloth bag slowly. Yes, on the clothes line, just like hanging out the laundry. Us kids were told to keep an eye on the cloth bag in case any unwanted birds decided to investigate. Who would be interested in checking this out as there was an odd smell coming from the bag?

Don't ask me about the flies. As a kid, I was more interested in playing than watching out for creatures. Maybe the flies weren't interested either.

Once the liquid stopped dripping, the curds would dry from the heat of the sun, and turn into a dry crumbly form ready for eating.

My parents came from two different cultures, so there would be a discussion who would eat it how? Dad ate his cottage cheese with cream and sugar, and mom ate hers with salt and pepper. There would be some conversation when it was time for the kids to choose, which way they were going to eat their cottage cheese. As for myself, I preferred the salt and pepper.

Cottage Cheese with Green Onion Salad

2 cups of cottage cheese – fresh
2 green onions – chopped

Mix together and serve.

****

Many times I have made changes to an ordinary recipe, especially salads, by adding or deleting ingredients to create something different for texture, flavor or color.

GRAVIES – SAUCES – DRESSINGS – STUFFING

Basic White Sauce

2 tbsps. margarine
2 tbsps. flour
1 cup milk
Pinch salt & pepper

Melt margarine in pan on medium heat. Add flour gradually, mixing until ingredient forms a soft crumbly texture. Do not scorch. Remove from heat, stir in milk until mixture is smooth, return to low heat and continue to stir until the mixture is creamy and thick with no lumps. Continue to cook until there is no taste of raw starch, season with salt and pepper to taste. Ready to pour over your favorite vegetable dish.

Brown Gravy

Cold Liquid Method-
Use a small glass jar with a tight fitting lid. Establish the amount of liquid to be thickened. For each measure of flour required use twice the quantity of water. Put flour and water into jar. Cover jar and shake vigorously. Stir mixture into hot liquid for gravy, stir until thick, smooth and there is no taste of raw starch. Add turkey, or ham or pot roast juices or liquid to flour and water mixture to make gravy. This method can also be used to thicken stews.

Creamed Fat Method-
A simple method to use when fat is soft.
1. Heat liquid until bubbles form
2. In a small bowl, blend fat and dry ingredient (flour)
3. Gather the mixture onto a spoon and stir into hot liquid, stir until thick, cook until no taste of raw starch remains.

By Scratch Method-
Remove meat from frying pan once cooked, then turn heat down to medium, sprinkle salt and pepper into pan of grease left over's from the fried meat. Add flour, one tablespoon at a time, stirring grease into flour mixture until all the grease is absorbed by the flour and the mixture turns into a golden brown crumbly texture. Add small portions of water gradually into the flour mixture and stir constantly, adding more water until liquid is a thick gravy. Can add more seasoning for taste. Gravy will take on the flavor of the meat.

141

Dill Sauce

2 tbsps. margarine
2 tbsps. flour
1 cup milk
2 tbsps. fresh chopped dill
Pinch salt & pepper

Melt margarine in pan on medium heat. Add flour gradually, mixing ingredients until combined, and forms a soft texture. Remove from heat, add dill and then stir in milk until mixture is smooth, return to heat on low and continue to stir until the mixture is creamy and thick with no lumps. Season with salt and pepper to taste. Ready to serve over cooked baby potatoes or other desired vegetables.

Cheese Sauce

2 tbsps. margarine
2 tbsps. flour
1 cup milk
¼ cup cheese (cheese whiz or grated cheddar cheese)
Pinch salt & pepper

Melt margarine and cheese in pan on medium heat. Add flour gradually, mixing ingredients until combined, forming a soft texture. Remove from heat, stir in milk until mixture is smooth, return to heat on low and continue to stir until the mixture is creamy and thick. Season with salt and pepper to taste. Ready to serve over cooked vegetables.

Sweet & Sour Sauce- One

1 cup white vinegar
1 ½ cups lightly packed brown sugar
¼ cup ketchup
1 tbsp. soya sauce
2 tbsps. cornstarch
Dash of salt
1 cup water
Dash of pepper
2 tbsps. water
14 oz. can pineapple chunks – optional

Drain pineapple syrup into a 4 cup bowl. Blend in water, vinegar, brown sugar, and ketchup and soya sauce. Pour into a sauce pan and cook over medium heat until mixture comes to a boil. Mix cornstarch and 2 tbsps. water together until dissolved. Stir about ¼ cup of hot mixture into cornstarch paste, blending well; add salt and pepper. Gradually stir this mixture back into the hot liquid mixture. Continue to cook for about 1 to 2 minutes on medium until the sauce is thickened. Stir constantly so the mixture doesn't burn. Add pineapple chunks if desired. Serve with cooked chicken, pork ribs or meatballs.
Makes 3 cups

Sweet & Sour Sauce – Two

2 tsps. corn starch
1 cup vinegar
1 cup water
1 ½ cups brown sugar
Pinch of pepper
Pinch of salt

Mix sugar, vinegar, salt and pepper. Heat until dissolved. Mix cornstarch and water to make a paste. Pour into liquid and let thicken, stirring constantly.
*pour sauce over browned spareribs and simmer for ½ hour.

Creamy Salad Dressing

½ cup sugar
¼ cup vinegar
1 tbsp. celery seed
1 tsp. dry mustard
1 cup miracle whip

Mix all ingredients together and whisk until well mixed

Auntie Edith Hall

Creamy Dressing

1 cup Miracle Whip
2 tbsps. white vinegar
Dash of Salt & pepper

Mix ingredients together until well mixed.

Spinach Salad Dressing

2 tbsps. sesame seeds
1 tbsp. poppy seeds
½ cup sugar
½ cup olive oil
¼ cup vinegar
¼ tsp. paprika
¼ tsp. Worcestershire sauce
1 tbsp. onion- minced

In a medium bowl, whisk together the sesame seeds, poppy seeds, sugar, olive oil, vinegar, paprika, Worcestershire sauce and onion. Cover and chill for one hour.

Cole Slaw Dressing

1 tbsp. white sugar
1 tsp. salt
½ tsp. dry mustard
¼ tsp. pepper
¼ cup vinegar
1 tbsp. oil

Mix dry ingredient together in small sauce pan. Add vinegar and oil. Bring to a boil, stirring constantly. Pour hot over 3 cups of finely shredded cabbage. Chill in refrigerator at least one hour before serving.

Japanese's Salad Dressing

1 pkg. noodles sauce
½ cup oil
2 to 4 tbsps. soya sauce
3 tbsps. vinegar
1 tbsp. white sugar
1 tsp. salt
½ tsp. pepper

In a glass bowl mix the dressing together until well stirred. Ready to pour over Japanese salad dry mixture.

Marinating Sauce

1/3 cup lemon juice
1/3 cup olive oil
1/3 cup red wine vinegar
Pinch of lemon pepper
Pinch of seasoned salt
2 garlic cloves- crushed

Mix together and pour over meat, ribs or chicken. Let stand for 2 to 3 hours, turning meat over occasionally. Ready for barbeque or bake.

****

Our son, Stephen took a trip to Vancouver with a friend, and stayed with the Donis family, an uncle to Stephen's friend. They were treated to a delicious meal using this marinating sauce recipe on chicken. Stephen, of course, asked for the recipe as he enjoys cooking, and this marinating sauce has become a special sauce used on chicken in his home.

Bread Stuffing

4 cups bread -cubes
3 tbsps. onions - chopped
1 tsp. salt
¼ tsp. pepper
¼ tsp. poultry seasoning
¼ tsp. sage
1/3 cup melted margarine
½ cup celery – optional
Water to moisten

Brown onions until tender in melted margarine, add salt, pepper, poultry seasoning and sage, stir well then pour over bread cubes and mix. Add cold water enough to make a moist mixture but not too wet. Ready to stuff a turkey or chicken.

White Margarine

Margarine originally came in a block form, similar to lard. The margarine was white and wrapped in wax type paper with a small packet filled with yellow powder and instructions.

I remember as a young girl, that my sisters or I would mix the yellow powder into the margarine, until the margarine turned a buttercup yellow, making sure there were no white streaks in the mixture. The margarine was then ready to be used.

How Did We Keep Food Cold on the Farm?

Years ago, there were different ways to keep food cold, when there was no electricity and no fancy fridges, as we have today.

In the early days, on the farm, we had no electricity, so our meals were made from the fresh vegetables in the garden and in the winter time, the meals were cooked from the canned vegetables and meats.

I remember the cooler, as we called it, was a large metal barrel with a lid, which was placed in a deep hole (the height of the barrel), and located near the back door of the house on the north side. Mom kept the milk, cream and a small amount of meat in this barrel, during the spring and summer months.

Anyone who had meat butchered would keep their meat in a freezer locker at the meat market in town.

Later years, mom had an ice box, (an insulated wood cabinet used for keeping food cool) which was placed in the kitchen. Food was not kept in this unit at any length of time. These ice boxes have a similarity as insulated bags, which we use today to transport foods.

In the early 60's, power was brought to our area and many of the farms were then hooked up to electricity. Mom and dad then purchased a deep freeze.

BREAKFAST – LUNCHEONS – DINNER DISHES

Pancake

1 ½ cups flour
1 to 2 tbsps. sugar
3 tsps. baking powder
½ tsp. salt
1 egg – beaten
1 ¾ cups milk
2 tbsps. oil
1 tsp. vanilla

Combine egg, milk, vanilla and oil together and stir, add dry ingredients and beat until combined. Pour pancake batter in hot frying pan or on a griddle, cook until batter is covered with bubbles. Turn pancake over and continue to bake until golden brown.
Makes about 12   pancakes.

****

Sunday was "Pancake Day" on the farm; the last pancake was specially made for our favorite old dog – Bugs, a black and white female Collie Cross. As my own family grew, the traditional pancakes and trimmings were served as Sunday Brunch.

Potato Pancakes

2 cups cooked mashed potatoes
1 ½ cups flour
1 egg- beaten
½ tsp. salt

Mix together well and roll dough on a floured surface, making the dough thin, less than a ¼". Cook slowly on a heated greased griddle, turning the pancake over once when golden brown.

****

Mom used a well-seasoned flat griddle heated on the wood cook stove. Each kid challenged the other as to how many pancakes they could eat. Mom made these on some Sunday's, and they were served with Rodgers syrup.

Sweet Milk Griddle Cakes

2 cups flour
1 tsp. salt
1 ½ tsps. baking powder
2 tbsps. sugar
2 cups milk
1 egg
1 tbsp. margarine- melted
1 tsp. vanilla

Mix flour, salt, baking powder and sugar. Add milk, vanilla, well beaten egg and margarine, mix well. Drop by tablespoons on a well-greased hot griddle, and brown on both sides. Serve hot with your favorite toppings.

Apple Pancake

1 ½ cups flour
1 to 2 tbsps. sugar
3 tsps. baking powder
½ tsp. salt
1 egg – beaten
1 ¾ cups milk
2 tbsps. oil
1 tsp. vanilla
1 apple – chopped finely

Combine egg, milk, vanilla and oil together and stir, add apple then dry ingredients and beat until combined. Pour pancakes batter in hot frying pan or on griddle, cook until batter is covered with bubbles. Turn pancake over and continue to bake until golden brown. Makes about 12 pancakes.

Waffles

1 ½ cups flour
2 tbsps. sugar
3 tsps. baking powder
½ tsp. salt
2 eggs- beaten
1 ½ cups milk
¼ cup melted margarine

Mix eggs, milk and margarine, add to the dry ingredients. Beat until smooth. Pour measured amount of batter on the hot waffle iron. Let it cook until done. Makes about 12 waffles
*great with whipped cream and fresh berries.

Crepes

8 eggs
½ cup flour
½ tsp. salt
2 cups milk

Beat eggs and salt together until light and foamy. Gradually stir in flour, add milk and blend well. In a well-greased heated cast iron pan, spread spoonfuls of mixture to cover bottom of pan. Cook on one side, then turn over and continue to cook. When done, roll up the crepe and place on a dish, keeping warm until ready to serve. Can sprinkle with brown sugar or your favorite jam or whipped cream

French Toast

2 eggs – slightly beaten
1 cup skim or whole milk
½ tsp. vanilla
½ tsp. ground cinnamon – optional
1/8 tsp. nutmeg- optional
¼ tsp. salt
2 tbsps. sugar
5 – 1" thick slices of bread – French, white or whole wheat

In a shallow bowl, using a wire whisk or a fork beat the eggs until foamy. Add milk, vanilla, salt, sugar, cinnamon and nutmeg. Beat well; set aside. Prepare oven at 200 degrees F. Lightly grease a large non-stick skillet and heat to medium heat. Dip bread slices one at time into the egg mixture, turning to coat and draining excess back into the dish. Place bread slices in prepared skillet. Cook until golden brown, turning once, about 1 to 2 minutes per side. Continue to cook the bread slices until all 5 slices are done. May need to add more oil to the skillet. Transfer cooked slices to a plate; keep warm in oven. Serve with lightly sprinkled cinnamon sugar and/or top with maple syrup or any desired topping.
Ready to eat.

Milk Toast

1 slice of bread
½ cup hot water
½ cup milk – canned evaporated milk
1 tsp. brown sugar
Jam

In a cereal bowl place a slice of bread. Pour hot water and milk over bread, then top with brown sugar or jam. Ready to eat

****

Milk Toast was one recipe we ate as kids and thought it quite delicious. We treated it like a dessert or a bedtime snack.

Porridge
1 Minute Rolled Oats

2/3 cups water
1/3 cup rolled oats
Dash of salt

Boil water and salt in covered sauce pan; stir in rolled oats, return to boil; reduce heat to simmer. Cook uncovered for 1 minute stirring constantly; remove from heat. Cover and let stand until desired thickness is reached. (For thicker porridge use less water and for thinner porridge use more water) Serve with cream and brown or white sugar, or add raisins or nuts or cinnamon or cut up apple.

Boiled Eggs

Soft-cooked-
Place eggs in a saucepan of cold water and heat slowly until boiling point is reached. Reduce heat and leave eggs in water 2 to 4 minutes, depending on desired softness of cooked eggs.

Hard-cooked-
Prepare same as for soft-cooked eggs. When water boils, reduce heat to keep water just below simmering. Cover and cook eggs 15 to 20 minutes. Cool at once in cold water to prevent dark surface on yolks.

Fried Eggs

Coat skillet with oil; place over medium heat. Add eggs and season with salt and pepper. When the whites of the eggs are set and edges cooked, cover and let cook until done to your liking.

Poached Eggs

Fill a frying pan ¾ full of water. Add pinch of salt. Bring to a boil. Break eggs and drop carefully into water. Turn heat down, cook until white is firm and there is a film over yolk. Remove each egg with a spatula with draining openings and place on toast. Ready to serve.
*to cook the white and yolks to your preference, use a tablespoon and scoop water onto each egg continuously until done.

Bacon & Eggs

Preheat a frying pan on medium heat and add bacon strips. Cook until done and/or crispy, turn over once. Ready to serve with fried eggs and toast.

Ham & Eggs

Preheat a frying pan on medium heat and add ham slices. Cook until done and/or lightly brown on each side, turn over once. Ready to serve with fried eggs and toast.

Scrambled Eggs & Bacon

For each egg allow 1 tbsp. milk, 1 tbsp. chopped bacon, and a pinch of salt and pepper to taste. Fry bacon lightly. Beat egg, milk and seasoning together. Add slightly beaten egg, milk, salt and pepper to bacon. Cook gently, stirring lightly. Just before removing from pan, add 1 tbsp. grated cheese if desired. This also makes ideal sandwiches.

Scrambled Egg & Onion

½ cup chopped onion
4 eggs
2 tbsps. milk
2 tbsps. margarine
1/8 tsp. pepper
½ tsp. salt

Fry chopped onion in oil slowly (do not burn). Mix the eggs, milk and seasoning until blended. Pour mixture over onion and cook slowly lifting occasionally from the bottom of the pan. When firm remove quickly from heat and serve. Great on toast or as a sandwich.

****

When I was growing up it was pancakes every Sunday or Sunday brunch as it is called today.

Raising my family, Sunday became much the same, everyone got up to bacon and eggs, and sometimes pancake brunch. This helped with the late risers, namely the teenagers in the house.

That's when; I became "Mom short order cook". Each child; three of them and hubby all preferred their bacon & eggs prepared differently.

One wanted egg over easy, one wanted hard fried egg, one wanted hard fried, but would only eat the white of the egg, and another wanted theirs sunny side up, not to runny. And the bacon crispy or not too crispy, oh and don't burn the toast!!

I figured that if I could handle all this in one sitting, maybe my patience and cooking experiences growing up helped. When it came to their eggs, I wasn't all that bad at whipping up a meal to please this particularly fussy family.

Now, with my grandchildren, it is much the same. "Grandma, the short order cook". It's scrambled eggs and a boiled egg or two. From mother to grandma, it makes no difference, I spoil everyone.

Omelet

4 eggs
Pinch salt
Pinch pepper
2 tbsps. milk

Fillings-
Bacon -diced cooked
Ham -chopped cooked
Mushrooms
Onion -chopped
Green Pepper
Tomatoes
Cheese -grated

Beat eggs until foamy, add salt, pepper and milk, and beat again. Preheat heavy skillet until hot, add 1 tbsp. oil, pour in half egg mix into pan and cook. As omelet cooks, lift edges with spatula, letting uncooked egg mixture run underneath until omelet is almost cooked, place sautéed filling and grated or sliced cheese on top of egg omelet; fold over, decrease heat, brown slightly underneath. Lift onto hot platter. Makes 2 servings.

Deviled Eggs

3 eggs – hard boiled
¼ tsp. salt
¾ tsp. prepared mustard
2 tbsps. mayonnaise
Dash of onion powder
Dash of pepper
2 to 3 drops Worcestershire sauce
Sprinkle of paprika, parsley or chives

Cut hard-boiled eggs in half, lengthwise. Remove yolks carefully from each egg half. Place all the yolks in a bowl and add remaining ingredients except mayonnaise and mix together until smooth and fluffy. Depending texture, add mayonnaise one tbsp. at a time until a desired mix. Fill each egg white half with mixture. Sprinkle with paprika or parsley or chives. Chill. Makes 6 halves.

Quiché –Spinach
No Shell

4 eggs - beaten
½ cup spinach – fresh chopped
¾ tsp. salt
¼ tsp. pepper
1 ½ cups milk
½ cup cheese- grated

Mix eggs, salt, pepper and milk together, beat until foamy. Place spinach on bottom of baking dish. Pour egg mixture over spinach and spread grated cheese on top. Bake in oven for 35 to 40 minutes at 350 degrees F.
*if using frozen spinach – need to drain off the water, by squeezing the spinach before using.

Sauerkraut

20 lbs. cabbage
½ lb. or 7 to 8 cup – coarse salt

Select firm, sound, mature heads of cabbage. Remove outer leaves; wash well. Quarter, remove core and slice very finely. Put 5 lbs. or about 7 ½ quarts shredded cabbage in a pan, add 2 ozs. or 3 ½ tbsps. salt and mix with hands. Then place cabbage in a crock container and tamp down firmly with wooden masher to extract juice and force out air. Repeat until all cabbage is used. Press down. Cover with a clean white cloth, then with a round wooden board small enough to fit down inside the crock, and then weigh down with a clean rock or brick. Keep cabbage covered while the brine that forms as the salt draws juice from cabbage. Keep in a warm place, 75 to 85 degrees F. Inspect each day, remove scum with a spoon and rinse cloth in clear water. The kraut will be fermented or cured in 10 to 20 days, depending upon the amount of cabbage and the temperature at which it is kept. Its appearance and taste will tell you when it is sufficiently cured. Kraut may be left in the crock to keep all winter, in a cold cellar or basement if care is taken to remove any scum that forms. It may be canned any time up to 1 to 3 months after fermentation is completed. Simply drain off juice, pack cold kraut into hot sterilized jars to ½ inch from top; heat juice to boiling, pour over kraut, seal and store in cool dark place. Do not process.

Large heads of cabbage from the garden were made into sauerkraut for the winter. Both my mom and mum Ireland made sauerkraut in stoneware crocks.

Fried Cabbage

While looking through many cook books, I didn't find a recipe for fried cabbage. Maybe because it was something no one thought would be tasty, or was an acquired taste.

However, it was my dad who cooked fried cabbage in our home. Perhaps it was from his background, nobody really knew for sure.

Chop a head of cabbage into medium bite size pieces and then place in a heated oiled frying pan cooking until tender. Adding salt, pepper and paprika. Stir often so the cabbage does not burn. Once the cabbage is transparent it is ready to be served.

Cabbage in Dough

*See Fried Cabbage recipe-

 Potato Dough-
4 potatoes - cooked and mashed
1 egg
3 tbsps. flour
Seasoning - salt and pepper

Mix potatoes, egg, seasoning and flour together to make soft dough. Add more flour if the dough is sticky. Sprinkle flour on a surface and roll out the dough, cutting into 4" x 4" squares. Place spoonful of fried cabbage in middle of the square, fold and pinch the edges. Place in an oiled frying pan and cook until lightly brown in color, turning over often, or place in oven at 350 degrees F and bake until lightly brown.

****

I tasted cabbage in dough, at my Uncle Mike Wurst's, another man who spent some time in the kitchen. Maybe his expertise at cooking was the result of being a bachelor for a number of years before marrying.

Boiled Cabbage

Remove outside leaves and wash cabbage. Cut in quarters and remove tough center core. Cut cabbage into pieces and cook quickly in a covered saucepan, using just enough boiling water to prevent from burning. Cooking time about 25 to 30 minutes, pending the amount of cabbage being cooked. Cook until tender and soft, drain, season with salt and pepper and margarine.

****

Making and/or eating cabbage rolls wasn't one of our family dishes while growing up. However, as the years passed, many old country recipes from European people were shared within the community. Today many of these dishes can be purchased ready made at the local grocery store or the farmer markets.

Dianne's Cabbage Rolls

1 cup rice
4 cups boiling water
1 tsp. salt
1/8 tsp. pepper
1 large onion or ¾ cup -chopped
3 sticks of celery – chopped - optional
1 ½ lbs. hamburger – beef or moose
1 can tomato soup or tomato paste
1 tsp. oil – vegetable or olive
1 medium green cabbage
1 can of canned tomatoes
1 can of tomato soup
4 tbsps. vinegar

Heat a frying pan over medium heat, add oil, add chopped onions and celery cooking until tender, add salt and pepper. Add hamburger, and cook meat until well done. Set aside. In a saucepan fill with water enough to boil rice. Bring water to a boil and add rice. Cook until done, stirring occasionally. (This is a quick way to prepare the rice filling for the cabbage rolls) Place meat on medium heat again, still in frying pan, add drained cooked rice, stir together, add 1 can of tomato soup, mix well. Check to see if the mixture requires more salt and pepper. Set aside to cool. Place large pan over medium heat, bring to a boil; dip whole cabbage in boiling water and turn occasionally until the cabbage leaves are tender and can be separated without breaking. Turn off heat. Cut each leave off at the core of the cabbage, place on a dish to cool. Once the whole cabbage has been stripped of its leaves, it's time to make cabbage rolls. Take a tablespoonful of rice filling and place on the bottom of the cabbage leaf, tuck the ends of the leaf inward and roll the leaf, keeping the filling inside. Once rolled, place in a baking dish or oven roasters, depending upon the number of rolls being made. Continue to roll the cabbage until all leaves and filling are used. The rolls will be different sizes. The cabbage rolls should be neatly and tightly place side by side, and layered in the pan. Mix one can of tomato soup and vinegar together, stirring until mixed. Pour over cabbage rolls. There should be enough liquid to cover the cabbage rolls half way up the dish. Then pour the canned tomatoes over the rolls. Cover with a lid. Bake 350 degrees F for 2 hours. Check occasionally making sure there is enough liquid in the pan so they do not burn.

Rice

Rice, another staple for many families, was purchased in various sized cloth bags. Today rice can be found in different sized containers or bags with a number of brand names and from different countries. The varieties today range from short, long, sushi, minute, brown, wild rice, and white.

In order to cook rice today, we need to follow the directions on the container or bag as each type of rice requires a certain length of cooking time.

****

There are many ways of making fried rice and we are one of those families.

My dad's fried rice was the most delicious and we always wanted at second helping. Dad made the hamburger tomato rice mixture and spiced it to perfection.

Hamburger & Tomatoes Fried Rice

1 tsp. salt
1 tsp. pepper
1 tsp. celery salt
1 tsp. onion salt
1 large onion- chopped
3 sticks of celery - chopped - optional
1 lb. hamburger - beef or moose
1 cup rice
1 can tomato soup
1 tsp. oil - vegetable or olive

In a frying pan and over medium heat, add oil, add chopped onions and celery cooking until tender, add salt, pepper, celery salt, onion salt and hamburger, cook meat until well done.
In a saucepan fill with water enough to boil rice. Bring water to a boil and add rice. Cook until done, stirring occasionally. Place meat on medium heat again, still in frying pan, add cooked rice, stir together, add 1 can of tomato soup, mix well. Check to see if the mixture requires more seasoning. Serve hot.

Chinese Rice

1 tsp. salt
1 tsp. pepper
1 tsp. celery salt
1 tsp. onion salt
1 medium onion- chopped
3 sticks of celery – chopped
1 can mushrooms – stems/pieces or fresh mushrooms
4 tbsps. soya sauce
1 tsp. oil
1 cup rice

Heat frying pan on medium heat, add oil, and add chopped onions and celery, cooking until tender, add salt, pepper, celery salt and onion salt, stirring to mix all the ingredients and spices together. Add mushrooms and soya sauce and stir again. Fill a saucepan with enough water to boil rice. Bring water to a boil and add rice. Cook until done, stirring occasionally. Add drained cooked rice to the mixture and stir until well mixed. Add 1 tbsp. soya sauce and mix.
Serve hot

Chicken Fried Rice

1 tsp. salt
1 tsp. pepper
1 tsp. celery salt
1 tsp. onion salt
2 tbsps. soya sauce
1 large onion- chopped
3 sticks of celery – chopped
1 cup chicken – cooked - diced
1 cup rice
2 tbsps. oil

Heat frying pan on medium heat, add oil, add chopped onions and celery sauté until tender, and add salt, pepper, celery salt and onion salt, stirring to mix all the ingredients and spices together. Add chicken and soya sauce, and stir again. Fill saucepan with enough water to boil rice. Bring water to a boil and add rice. Cook until done, stirring occasionally. Add drained, cooked rice to the mixture and stir until well mixed. Add 1 tbsp. soya sauce and mix. Serve hot

Fried Rice & Ham

1 tsp. salt
1 tsp. pepper
1 tsp. celery salt
1 tsp. onion salt
2 tbsps. soya sauce
1 large onion- chopped
3 sticks of celery – chopped
1 cup ham - cooked
1 cup rice
2 tbsps. oil

In a frying pan use medium heat, add oil, add chopped onions and celery sauté until tender, and add salt, pepper, celery salt and onion salt, stirring to mix all the ingredients and spices together. Add ham and soya sauce and stir again. Fill a saucepan with enough water to boil rice. Bring water to a boil and add rice. Cook until done, stirring occasionally. Add cooked rice to the mixture and stir until well mixed. Add 1 tbsp. soya sauce and mix. Serve hot.

Boiled Rice

2 cups water
½ cup rice
Pinch of salt

In a sauce pan bring water to a boil, add rice and salt and stir occasionally until rice is tender. Drain water and serve rice plain as a side dish.
*can serve rice plain as a side dish
*or add to plain rice -raisins, cream and sprinkle with sugar – white or brown

Kedagree –Scottish

1 ½ cups rice - boiled
2 eggs - boiled
1 salmon - 7 oz. can
1 tbsp. margarine
Salt, pepper, curry

Heat water in a sauce pan, bringing to a boil add rice and cook until done. Set aside to cool. Boil eggs until hard boiled. Cool. Mix rice, chopped eggs and salmon together. Add salt, pepper and curry to taste. Bake in oven for 10 minutes at 350 degrees F.
Ready to serve

****

Kedagree was unknown to me, but not to my husband Jim. This is an old Scottish dish, which his mother Betty, a war bride from New Cumnock, Scotland, made for her family all the time. I was first introduced to Kedgeree at Jim's parent's home.

Hamburger Mushroom & Noodle Goulash

1 lb. hamburger - beef
1 can mushroom soup
1 can mushroom stems/pieces or fresh
1 onion - chopped
3 sticks celery - chopped -optional
½ tsp. salt
½ tsp. pepper
½ tsp. celery salt
1 tbsp. oil
2 cups egg noodles

Heat frying pan on medium heat, add oil, and add chopped onions and celery sauté until tender add salt, pepper, celery salt and hamburger. Cook meat until well done. Add mushrooms and mushroom soup, stir in until well mixed. In boiling water cook noodles until tender. Add noodles to the meat mushroom mixture and stir. Ready to serve.

Vegetable Marrow with Hamburger & Rice

Hamburger/Rice Filling-
1 tsp. salt
1 tsp. pepper
1 tsp. celery salt
1 tsp. onion salt
1 large onion- chopped
3 sticks of celery - chopped - optional
1 lb. hamburger - beef or moose
1 cup rice
1 can tomato soup
1 tsp. oil - vegetable or olive

Take a frying pan and heat over medium heat, add oil, add chopped onions and celery cooking until tender, add salt, pepper, celery salt, onion salt and hamburger, cook meat until well done. In a saucepan fill with water enough to boil rice. Bring water to a boil and add rice. Cook until done, stirring occasionally. Place meat on medium heat again, still in frying pan, add cooked rice, stir together, add 1 can of tomato soup, mix well. Check to see if the mixture requires more seasoning.

Vegetable Marrow-
Wash marrow, split in half and remove seeds, making a hollow length wise in both halves, like a boat shape. Add hamburger and rice filling into the hollow of the marrow. Pour tomato soup and season over filling. Place ½ cup of water in a rectangle cake pan. Lay both halves side by side in pan. Bake at 350 degrees F about 1 hour. Cover marrow with foil so top doesn't burn.

Hamburger Tomato Goulash

1 lb. hamburger - beef or moose
1 can tomato soup
1 onion - chopped
½ tsp. salt
½ tsp. pepper
½ tsp. celery salt
1 tbsp. oil

Heat frying pan over medium heat, add oil, add chopped onions sauté until tender, and add salt, pepper, celery salt and hamburger. Cook meat until well done. Add tomato soup, stir in until well mixed.
Serve hot over mashed potatoes.

Mushroom Meat Balls

1 lb. hamburger - beef or moose
1 can mushroom soup
1 can mushroom stems/pieces or fresh- optional
1 onion - chopped
½ tsp. seasoning salt
1 tbsp. oil
1 egg
½ cup rolled oats or crushed crackers

Mix together meat, onion, egg, rolled oats or crackers and seasoning salt until well mixed. Take meat mixture and make small 1" balls. In a frying pan; heat over medium heat, add oil, add meat balls and cook until brown, turning occasionally. Pour mushroom soup and mushrooms over the meat balls and stir until liquid is well mixed, and is well heated or bubbles.
Ready to serve.

Hamburger Patties

1 ½ lbs. hamburger - beef or moose
1 onion - chopped
1 tsp. seasoning salt
1 tbsp. oil
1 egg
½ cup rolled oats or crushed crackers

Mix together meat, onion, egg, rolled oats or crackers and seasoning salt until well mixed. Take meat mixture and make patties. In a frying pan; heat over medium heat, add oil, add patties and cook until brown and well done, turning occasionally.
Other ways to cook-
-Barbeque; brush with barbeque sauce
-George Forman grill

Meat Loaf

1 ½ lbs. hamburger - beef or moose
1 onion - chopped
½ tsp. seasoning salt
1 egg
¾ cup rolled oats or crushed crackers
½ cup ketchup

Mix together meat, onion, egg, rolled oats or crackers and seasoning salt until well mixed. Place mixed meat in a loaf pan and pour ketchup over the top of loaf. Bake in oven at 375 degrees F for about 45 to 55 minutes or until done.

Chili

1 lb. hamburger - beef or moose
1 medium onion - chopped
2 celery stalks - chopped
2 tbsps. oil
1 can pork n beans
1 can mushrooms- sliced
1 can kidney beans
1 can stewed tomatoes
1 tsp. salt
½ tsp. pepper
2 tsps. chili spice or 1 pkg. chili seasoning
1 can tomato soup

Heat large skillet, add oil then onion, celery to sauté and then add hamburger and cook until well done. Stirring occasionally; add pork n beans, mushrooms, kidney beans, tomato soup, stewed tomatoes and seasonings. Continue cooking on medium heat until the chili is hot and thick. May want to add extra chili spice for a spicier flavor.

****

Our oldest son Robert preferred to cook Chili, and he seemed to know how to make it just right for the family.

Nacho & Cheese

Pending size of plateful desired

12 to 20 Nacho Chips
½ cup cheese - grated or sliced
½ cup salsa sauce
½ cup sour cream
2 tbsps. olives -sliced - optional
½ tomatoes - chunks -optional

Arrange nacho chips on a plate, layering with cheese. Sprinkle sliced olives and tomato chunks over the top of the chips if desired. Heat in micro-wave until cheese is melted. Serve with a side dish of salsa sauce and sour cream.

Taco & Cheese with Hamburger

1 wrap -any flavor
½ cup cheese - grated
¼ cup taco sauce
¼ cup sour cream
2 tbsps. olives-sliced
½ tomato- chunks
1 cup hamburger - cooked
¼ cup onion - diced
6 lettuce leaves -cut into bite size pieces
2 tbsps. oil

Heat skillets on medium heat; add oil, and onions and sauté. Add hamburger, salt and pepper and taco sauce, stir occasionally until meat is well done. Set aside to cool. Place a wrap in a taco baking bowl and bake in the oven at 350 degrees F for about 7 minutes or until wrap is puffed, crispy and light brown. Gently remove baked wrap from taco baking bowl and set on a plate. Fill by layering, lettuce, hamburger, tomato, olives and cheese. Top with sour cream and taco sauce if desired. Ready to serve one.

Spaghetti & Meat Balls

Meat Ball-
1 lb. hamburger – beef or moose
½ cup onion – chopped
1 tsp. seasoning salt
1 tbsp. oil
1 egg
½ cup rolled oats or crushed crackers

Mix together meat, onion, egg, rolled oats or crackers and seasoning salt until well mixed. Take meat mixture and form bite size balls. In a frying pan; heat over medium heat, add oil and meat balls and cook until brown and well done, turning occasionally.

Spaghetti Sauce
1 can - 10 oz. spaghetti sauce
2 tbsps. cheddar cheese or cheese whiz

2 cups cooked spaghetti

Mix sauce and cheese together, pour over meat balls, and cook on low heat for 15 minutes. Serve with cooked spaghetti.

Beef Roast with Vegetables

1 beef roast
4 potatoes - cut in half
6 carrots - cut in half
1 onion - sliced
Salt & pepper

Place roast into a roasting pan, add about 2 cups of water and cook in oven at 350 degrees F for the required time, depending upon size of roast. About one hour into the cooking, add the vegetables and seasoning. Cook until roast is done and vegetables are tender. Can make gravy from the liquid if desired.

See Gravy recipe-

Swiss Steak

1 ½ lbs. steak - round
1/3 cup flour
1 medium onion - chopped
½ tsp. salt
1/8 tsp. pepper
2 tbsps. oil
1 can tomato soup
½ cup water

Cut meat into 2" pieces. Mix flour, salt and pepper together, dip steak pieces into flour mixture coating on both sides. Heat skillet pan on medium heat, add oil then add steak chunks and onions to brown. Pour can of tomato soup and water over steak and onions; continue to simmer until meat is tender. Add more water if needed during cooking. The liquid can be thickened with a flour paste for gravy if desired.

See Gravy recipe-

Fried Steak & Onions

3 lbs. steak - any type of cut
1 large onion - sliced
1 tsp. salt
1/8 tsp. pepper
1 cup flour
2 tbsps. oil

Mix salt, pepper and flour together in a bowl. Dip steak into flour mixture, covering both sides. Heat skillet pan on medium heat, add oil then add steak, browning on both sides. Add onions and stir until onions are tender. Continue to cook steak to perfection. Serves 6

Lasagna with Garlic Bread

9 lasagna noodle
2 cans tomato soup or 8 oz. tomato paste
1 cup cheese- cheddar
2 lbs. hamburger
½ cup onion - chopped
¼ tsp. pepper
½ tsp. salt
1 tsp. oregano
Oil

Cook lasagna noodles accordingly to package directions, do not add salt. In a heavy skillet, sauté onions, add hamburger cook until well done. Stir in pepper, salt, oregano, add tomato soup or paste and stir well. Drain noodles in a colander. Place layer of noodles on bottom of a 13" x 9" baking dish, pour hamburger mixture over noodles, top with slices of cheese and continue to repeat the layers. Top with a layer of cheese. Bake for 45 minutes at 350 degrees F.

Crusty Garlic Bread-
2 small loaves - Italian or French
Preheat oven 350 degrees F. Cut each loaf crosswise into diagonal slices, without cutting all the way through. Brush cut sides of slices with garlic butter mix (garlic salt and margarine) Fold and wrap each loaf in foil, place on a baking sheet. Bake until heated through about 10 to 15 minutes. Unwrap the loaves, slice and place on a bread board or in a basket.
Serve immediately.

Meat Pie

1 ½ lbs. beef or moose hamburger
3 tbsps. olive oil
3 tbsps. flour
1 large onion – diced
6 carrots –chopped
5 potatoes – cut into cubes
3 sticks of celery – sliced – optional
Salt & pepper
Parsley & celery salt
1 cube of beef oxo
½ cup water
Pastry – see recipe

Using a frying pan, heat on medium heat, add oil, and add chopped onions and celery sauté until tender add salt, pepper, celery salt, parsley and hamburger, cooking meat until well done. Stirring occasionally. Add vegetables and water. In small bowl mix beef oxo and flour together with a small amount of water to make a gravy mix. Add to vegetables and simmer on medium heat until vegetables are tender and liquid is a thick gravy paste. May need to add more seasoning for taste. Once cooked, let cool to lukewarm. Prepare pastry dough. Place dough on bottom of a baking dish, pour in meat mixture, cover top with another rolled out pastry dough covering the meat mixture. Seal edges by pinching the dough together. Indent several markings with a fork on top of dough. Bake at 350 degrees F for about 25 minutes until the crust is golden brown. Serves 6

Quick & Tasty Wiener Rolls

6 wieners
1 container of wiener wraps
6 slices of cheese- optional

Unwrap dough, stretching dough, cutting the indented seam, place a wiener and slice of cheese, if desired on dough strip and roll up the dough. Place wiener wraps on a greased baking sheet. Bake 6 wieners at 375 degrees F for 10 to 15 minutes until golden brown. Turn over once while baking.

Fried Liver & Onions with Bacon

1 lb. beef liver- fresh
½ tsp. salt
1/8 tsp. pepper
¼ cup flour
1 onion- chopped
8 slices of bacon

Rinse beef liver, dry with paper towel, cut into 1" thin strips. In a separate bowl mix together flour, salt and pepper. Take each liver strip and roll into flour mix. Preheat skillet with oil and once heated place liver into pan and begin cooking on medium heat. Once liver is browned turn over and brown other side, add bacon slices and onions and continue to cook; mixing the liver, bacon and onion together. Turn heat down and continue to cook on low until bacon and onions are cooked. Ready to serve hot.

Sauerkraut & Wieners

2 cups sauerkraut
3 wieners -whole or cut-up

Place sauerkraut into a sauce pan and heat with a small amount of water in the bottom of pan. Heat on medium heat until sauerkraut is hot, add wieners and mix. Continue to cook until wieners are cooked and increased in size. Ready to serve.
*can eat as a serving or fill a hotdog bun with sauerkraut and a wiener, add mustard and ready for a delicious tasty bun.

Beefsteak & Kidney Pie

Meat Filling-
1 ½ lbs. beefsteak
½ lb. beef kidney
1 tbsp. flour
1 tsp. salt
¼ tsp. pepper
1/8 tsp. nutmeg
1 cup beef stock

Split kidney; remove core, tough skin, and hard matter. Cut into 2" pieces. Cover with cold, salt water for 1 hour. Drain. Cut beef steak into 2" pieces. Sprinkle beef and kidney with flour, salt, pepper and nutmeg. Line the sides of a greased baking dish with pie pastry. Mix beef and kidney together. Place in dish. Add beef stock. Cover meat with pastry. Bake in oven at 350 degrees F for 1 ½ hours.
Serves 4 to 6

****

Some memories never leave you and this one has stuck with me for years. My very first meal at my relatives to-be and not knowing anything about their family cultures or traditions was an adventure. Jim's mother was accustomed to making this dish often. She may have not known that this would be a different meal for me. Unfamiliar with different foods and flavors, my taste buds didn't joyfully respond to eating KIDNEY? Using the manners I had been taught, I accepted and ate the meal. However, I never forgot it nor served this to my own family. Actually, I think my husband was okay with this, because he didn't particularly like this dish. Sorry mum!

Egg Rolls

Filling-
4 cups shredded cabbage
½ cup chopped onions
½ cup chopped celery
2 tsps. salt
1 cup diced cooked chicken or meats or shrimp
1 tsp. soya sauce
1 tsp. oil – peanut
½ tsp. pepper
1 can bean sprouts
1 pkg. won ton wraps

Combine vegetables in a deep bowl with salt. Let stand for 15 minutes. Drain, add other ingredients and mix well. Place about 2 tbsps. filling mixture in the center of each square won ton wrap. Brush edges of wrap lightly with beaten egg. Overlap to opposite side of filling and press to seal. Press ends firmly to close opening and deep fry.

How to fry egg rolls –
Deep fry in 2" of oil at 375 degrees F, in small quantities until golden brown.

To Freeze-
Fry as above cooking for 3 minutes only. Wrap cooled egg rolls in heavy tin foil and store in freezer. When needed, thaw and fry again for 3 to 4 minutes.

Spaghetti & Tomato Sauce with Sausage

Spaghetti
1 can tomatoes - stewed or homemade
1 tbsp. oil
¼ cup onion - diced
¼ cup celery - diced
Salt & pepper
6 sausages -beef & onion

Cook sausages in a skillet or George Forman grill until cooked. Cook spaghetti accordingly to package directions. Preheat a skillet on medium heat and add oil, then add onions and celery to sauté. Mix together spaghetti, tomatoes, sauté vegetables and seasoning. Add sausages and serve.

Sausage Rolls

1 ½ lbs. pork sausage meat
1 onion – finely chopped
3 eggs
1 tbsp. oil
Salt
Pepper
Flaky Pastry

Pour oil in a frying pan; add onions and sauté until tender. Place the sausage meat into a large mixing bowl, with the onion, two eggs and seasoning. Mix until all the ingredients are thoroughly and evenly mixed. On a lightly floured surface, roll out half the pastry to an 8" x 10" rectangle. Cut length wise into 2 strips. Repeat with the remaining pastry. Form the sausage meat into 4 long sausages the length of the pastry strips. Place each sausage into the center of each pastry strip. Beat the third egg in a small bowl and lightly brush the edges of the pastry with the beaten egg. Fold the pastry over the meat filling to form two long rows then flip the sausage roll over so the seam is underneath. Brush the top surface lightly with beaten egg. Cut the rolls into 1 ½" length – you can vary the length to the style of roll you want. For a canapé size you may want to make tiny rolls. Place the sausage rolls on a greased baking pan and bake for 20 minutes at 400 degrees F or until golden brown.

See Flaky Pastry recipe-

****

Sausage rolls were first introduced to me when I married into the Ireland family. As you may have noticed, while reading these stories, that I was introduced to many new foods and flavors. Mum Ireland always made sausage rolls at Christmas time, one of their family special traditions. When mum moved to Calgary, she continued making sausage rolls for our family. A special gift package would always arrive on the Greyhound Bus just before Christmas. Our sausage rolls had arrived! They were a great treat for us and a joy to receive.

German Fried Potatoes

Wash and pare potatoes and slice very thin. Soak them in cold water 1 hour. Drain and dry thoroughly. Put a small amount of oil in a frying pan and heat on medium. Add potatoes, sprinkle with salt, cover with a tight fitting lid. Fry slowly until tender and brown, turning occasionally to prevent burning. Allow 1 medium potato per serving.
*can add chopped onions with potatoes while cooking and sprinkle with paprika.

Potato Puffs

½ cup flour
1 ½ tsps. baking powder
½ tsp. salt
1 cup cooked mashed potatoes
2 eggs

Mix flour, baking powder and salt together. Blend into mashed potatoes. Mix again and add beaten eggs. Stir thoroughly. Drop by spoonful into hot grease. Fry until golden brown on both sides.

Potato Chunks

4 medium potatoes or sweet potatoes - cut into large wedges
1 tbsp. olive oil
½ tsp. seasoning salt
2 garlic cloves - minced - optional

Place potato wedges in a large bowl; add cold water to cover. Let stand for 5 minutes. Prepare oven to 425 degrees F. Grease non-stick baking sheet with olive oil or spray. Set aside. Drain potatoes, spread on a paper towel to dry. Transfer potatoes to a clean large bowl, sprinkle with oil, and seasoning salt; toss gently to combine mixture. Arrange seasoned potatoes on baking sheet and bake for 20 minutes, turning after 10 minutes for even browning. Serve hot.

Potato Patties

2 cups cooked and mashed potatoes
½ cup onion- chopped - optional
½ tsp. salt
½ tsp. pepper
1 cup flour
1 egg

Mix all ingredients together until well mixed. If the mixture is too sticky add more flour. On a floured surface, place potato mixture and add more flour until the dough becomes soft and easy to handle. Form into patty's and place in an oiled heated frying pan. Cook until golden brown, turning once. Can be served with bacon and eggs.
 Serve hot.

Scallop Potatoes

2 cups potatoes - slices
1 tsp. salt
½ tsp. pepper
2 cups milk
2 tbsps. flour
1 tbsp. margarine
½ onions -chopped - optional
½ cup grated cheese - optional

Grease baking dish with margarine, arrange sliced potatoes into dish, sprinkle with salt, pepper, and add onion, cheese and flour. Dot with margarine. Repeat process until all ingredients used. Add milk to cover potatoes. Grate cheese over top and cover with lid. Bake 400 degrees F for 25 minutes. Allow one potato per serving.

Potato Chips

Peel potatoes. Cut crosswise, in very thin slices. Let stand, covered in icy water, 45 minutes. Drain and dry between towels. Fry in deep fat at 325 degrees F until golden brown. Drain off oil on unglazed paper. Sprinkle with salt if desired.

****

My mother-in-law made potato chips often and the whole family enjoyed them. However, just add ketchup, and don't count the calories!

Potatoes & Mushroom & Onions - Barbequed

4 medium potatoes - cut into large wedges
1 can mushrooms - stems/pieces
1 medium onion - sliced
1 tbsp. margarine
¼ tsp. ground black pepper
½ tsp. seasoning salt
2 garlic cloves - minced - optional

Lay out a piece of foil about 2' x 2', spread margarine on foil, and then place potatoes, onion and mushrooms on foil, sprinkle with seasoning. Fold foil covering the vegetables, making sure there are no openings (to prevent leakage). Ready for the barbeque. Cook on grill until done, test with a fork.

Baked Potato with Onion Soup Mix

Take one whole washed potato and split in half. Spread margarine on one potato half then add 1 tbsp. onion soup mix. Put potato together and wrap in foil, ready for the barbeque. Cook on grill until done, testing with a fork

Loaded Baked Potato
Oven Style

Select medium size potatoes. Wash with a vegetable brush to remove all particles of dirt. Soak in cold water 1 hour. Bake at 400 degrees F in oven for 40 to 50 minutes or until soft. Once baked, remove from oven and split in half, spread with margarine, add sour cream, cooked bacon crumbs, chopped green onions and serve.
*may want to sprinkle grated cheese on top

Loaded Baked Potato
Micro-Wave Style

Select medium size potatoes. Wash with a vegetable brush to remove all particles of dirt. Soak in cold water 1 hour. Bake in micro-wave for 10 to 15 minutes or until soft. Once baked, remove and split in half, spread with margarine, add sour cream, cooked bacon crumbs, chopped green onions and serve.

*may want to sprinkle grated cheese on top.

Creamed Peas & Carrots

2 tbsps. Margarine
2 tbsps. Flour
Salt & pepper
2 cups milk
2 ½ cups peas & carrots – pre-cooked

Melt margarine in a sauce pan on low heat, add flour and stir until well mixed. Season with salt and pepper. Add milk stirring constantly, ensuring no lumps form and until the mixture bubbles. Add cooked peas and carrots. Stir thoroughly. Serve hot

Cheese Whiz Cauliflower

1 medium head of cauliflower

Fill medium size sauce pan half full of water and bring to a boil. Add cauliflower pieces and cook until tender. Drain and set aside. Using the cheese sauce, pour over cauliflower, stir gently and serve hot.

See Cheese Sauce recipe-

Fried Carrots

Select long straight carrots. Wash with a vegetable brush to remove all particles of dirt, and then peel with a peeler. Cut length wise. Preheat skillet on low heat, add oil, and then add carrots, laying them flat in the skillet. Turn carrots more than once, to ensure not to burn. When carrots are tender and lightly browned, season with salt and pepper. Ready to serve.

****

Dad was famous at making this dish. He knew how to cook the carrots tender and not scorch them.

Corn Fritters

Fritter Batter-
1 ½ cups flour
2 tsps. baking powder
¾ tsp. salt
1 cup milk
1 egg
2 cans of kernel corn

Mix egg, milk, salt, baking powder and flour together and beat until smooth. Add corn to the batter and mix well.

Fry Fritters-
Heat oil in deep fryer to 375 degrees F. Take a tablespoonful of fritter batter and drop into hot oil. As soon as the fritters rise to the top, turn them over. When fritters are a rich brown shade, about 3 minutes, lift from the oil and drain on absorbent paper before placing them on a serving dish. Fritters are normally irregular in shape and this adds to their appeal. Cooked fritters can be served with your favorite jam or eaten plain. Makes about 18.

Another, first experience tasting corn fritters at my in-law's. At the time I thought it was odd to eat corn in a batter with jam. To my surprise, they were delicious, as Jim had said. They were one of his favorite foods.

****

Growing up, all I knew was that the corn at the market gardens along Shaftesbury Trail was ready to be picked before the corn was ready in our garden on the farm. And to my knowledge it had no particular brand name associated with it.

However, in later years, my husband and I learned about different brand names of corn, while visiting mum Ireland in Calgary. We had taken mum to the shopping center to pick up a few groceries for supper. As we were about to get into our vehicle, mum made a remark that we should get some peaches and cream. What! We were just in the store. Jim and I looked at each other; not knowing what mum's plan was, thinking she wanted to get a dessert. Mum jumped out of the car and started across the parking lot. We said out loud, "peaches and cream!" We followed her, to an outside vender who was selling fresh corn. Mum bought a few cobs of corn and we feasted on corn that night. Now we know peaches and cream is CORN!

Fried Onion Rings

Cut large onions crosswise into 1/3" to 1/4" thick slices. Separate into rings. Dry onion thoroughly, coat with flour. Using tongs – dip each ring into a fritter batter, letting excess drip off. Deep fry a few at time in ½" to 1" deep hot oil. Cook until golden brown about 2 minutes. Drain on absorbent paper.

See Fritter Batter recipe-

Spaghetti & Cheese

Spaghetti -pending servings
Salt & pepper
1 tbsp. margarine
2 tbsps. Cheese Whiz

Cook spaghetti accordingly to package directions. Drain spaghetti and add margarine, cheese whiz, salt and pepper. Mix well.

Homemade Egg Noodles

3 egg yolks
1 whole egg
3 tsps. cold water
1 tsp. salt
2 cups flour

Beat egg yolks and egg well; add water and beat mixture; add salt and stir. Add flour gradually and mix in until the dough is stiff, kneading the dough mixture. Roll dough thin on a floured surface. Cut in narrow strips   1/8" to ½" wide. Ready to drop into hot soup.

Homemade Baked Pork & Beans

2 cups white navy beans
6 cups water
½ lb. salt pork or pork hocks-cut in cubes
1 cup chopped onion
1 tsp. salt
Pinch of pepper
1 tsp. dry mustard
¼ cup brown sugar
¼ cup ketchup
1 cup molasses
2 tbsps. vinegar

Wash white navy beans and soak overnight in enough water to cover and 1 tsp. of salt. Drain. Brown pork hock chunks and onions. Fill a large pot with 6 cups of water, add browned pork hocks, onion and beans and bring to a boil, and then simmer for 30 minutes. Combine remaining ingredients, stir well. Cover and cook on medium heat for 5 to 7 hours, adding more water if needed. Stir occasionally.
*can use a crock pot or slow cooker. (cook for 6 hours)

Fried Bologna

Slice bologna in ½" thickness and place in an oiled heated skillet and fry, turning over once to brown evenly on both sides. Ready to serve.

****

Does anyone remember these days when fried bologna was part of the meal? Today, fried bologna is still being served on the menu at Smittys Restaurant, in St. Johns, New Foundland.

****

The story was that, bologna was always called steak. Going to have steak tonight, meant a big hunk of fried bologna.

Roast Chicken

1 whole roasting chicken
Salt and pepper

Prepare stuffing and insert mixture inside of chicken. Place chicken in the roaster, add about 2 cups of water. Sprinkle salt and pepper over top of chicken breast. Roast chicken at 350 degrees F. until browned and cooked. Roasting time pending size of chicken.

See Stuffing recipe-

Fried Chicken – Country Style

1 whole frying chicken
Salt, pepper, paprika
1 cup flour
4 or 5 tbsps. Oil

Cut up chicken into parts. Mix flour and seasonings together in a bowl. Preheat a frying pan on medium heat and add oil. Roll chicken parts into flour mixture. Place into frying pan and fry chicken until well uniformly browned, turning occasionally. Monitor heat level, so as not to burn. Chicken should be golden brown and crispy, ready to serve.

Sunday Supper on the Farm
"Fried Chicken"

On the farm, Sunday suppers were fried chicken. As on most farms, chickens were raised to lay eggs and butchered for meat.

Preparing for Sunday supper would be an all-day occurrence, when it came to butchering and preparing a chicken for a meal.

First a chicken would be selected from the chickens in the chicken coop, usually the biggest, fattest, and had to be the right age. Whatever that meant! First dad checked out his axe blade, making sure it was good and sharp. Then dad would come with the chicken of his choice, holding it by the feet, upside down. The chickens never seemed to squawk much. He laid the chicken's neck on the wood chopping block and with one strike with the axe, cut off its head. He would lay the chicken on the ground, and then the headless chicken would bounce and jump all over. If you were standing too close, you almost thought the chicken was chasing you, as it moved different directions. This only lasted for a few minutes.

Next it was time to pluck the feathers, remove the insides and clean the chicken completely. This is one job, I didn't care for. The chicken was dipped into hot water so the feathers would come out easily. Once the feathers and pin feathers (small tiny feathers under the skin) were removed, the chicken was singed over an open fire to remove any remaining feathers. Then the chicken was opened up to remove all the internal inner parts, what we called guts, then dipped into cold water, and washed inside and out. Now the chicken was ready to be cooled, and was left to soak in cold water for the rest of the day until it was time to be cooked for supper.

Looking back, this was a normal occurrence, on the farm. However, when this is described to the younger generation of today, they are horrified, and I am sure they will never look at Kentucky Fried Chicken the same way again.

Ordering Chicks from the Catalogue

When spring came around, usually at Easter time, mom would place an order through a mail order catalogue for her chickens from Rumble's Hatchery in Peace River, Alberta. She would order a certain breed and specific number of chickens.

Then, in a few weeks' time, mom and dad would bring home a couple of card board boxes full of peeping fuzzy yellow chicks. These boxes were placed on the floor near the wood cook stove for warmth. The chicks were kept in the kitchen for a few days or longer, depending on weather, so there was a lot of noisy peeping day and night. Once the weather warmed up, the chicks, now a bit older were moved to the barn into an area designated for the chicks, so they couldn't escape.

A chick feeder for food and water was then set up. This had to be monitored several times a day to ensure the chicks were eating.

As these little yellow creatures grew, they changed color and feathers started to appear. Once the chicks were older, they were moved to the chicken coop with the older hens and rooster.

Sometimes at Easter, the chicks were colored pink and blue. I remember, one time years back, some of these colored chicks did arrive in these boxes that came to our place.

Sweet & Sour Spareribs

Prepare 1 ½ lbs. spareribs (cut small) by placing ribs into a pan of boiling water and boil until ribs are almost cooked. Drain off water and place ribs in an oiled frying pan to brown. Continue to cook slowly until very tender. Drain off any excess fat.

Sweet & Sour Sauce-
½ cup water
½ cup brown sugar
¼ cup vinegar
¼ cup ketchup
1 tbsp. soya sauce
1 tbsp. cornstarch
Pineapple chunks – optional

Combine water, brown sugar, vinegar, ketchup and soya sauce in a sauce pan and heat on medium. Mix cornstarch with 2 tbsps. of water and stir well until mixture is smooth. Add to liquid and stir until thickened. Pour over ribs and simmer for ½ hour. Serves 4.
*can serve ribs without sauce and pour sauce over ribs of one's choice.

Crock Pot Ribs

Cut 1 ½ lbs. of spareribs into pieces (4 ribs per piece). Place into crock pot. Add 1 cup of water and turn crock pot on high. Pour 4 tbsps. barbeque sauce over the ribs. Cook for about 5 hours. Remove ribs from crock pot and place on a grilling pan. Turn oven to broil. Brush more barbeque sauce on each rib piece or use another favorite sauce. Broil until golden brown and then turn ribs over, add more sauce then broil again until golden brown. Ready to serve.

Pork Chop & Mushrooms

Place pork chops in a heated oiled skillet and brown on both sides, turning over once. Add salt and pepper to season. Once pork chops are done, pour a can of mushroom soup over the pork chops and simmer for about half hour.

Pork Chops – Hungarian Style

Dip chops in flour and brown on both sides in a little hot oil. Season with salt and pepper and sprinkle with paprika. Scatter caraway seeds over the chops and pour ½ cup water around them. Cover skillet and cook slowly until chops are tender (about 1 hour) Add small quantities of water during cooking period to keep chops from drying out. Can make gravy from liquid.

Mrs. Ed. (Margaret) Hededus - dad's cousin

See Liquid Gravy Method recipe-

Roast Turkey

Roast turkey – stuffed or not stuffed, in oven at the required temperature and time depending the size of the turkey. Can make turkey gravy from the liquid if desired.

See Liquid Gravy Method recipe-

****

I have many wonderful memories of special family celebrations, especially at Christmas. A turkey dinner with all the trimmings and our traditional Christmas pudding. Actually this is my favorite time, to spend in the kitchen, cooking an elegant dinner; setting the table with our best dinnerware, sparkling glasses, candles, and decorative glittery holiday center pieces.

Yorkshire Pudding

1 cup flour
1 cup milk
1 tsp. salt
3 eggs

Beat smooth flour, milk, salt; add eggs separately, beating till smooth after each egg. Let stand. Prepare muffin tin by putting 3 tbsps. of hot drippings from roast in each cup. Spoon in batter about ¾ full. Bake at 350 degrees F for about 30 minutes. Each Yorkshire pudding will rise above the muffin cup and when cooked gently remove and serve hot with roast and vegetables with gravy.

****

Mum Ireland made Yorkshire pudding to perfection. A very delicious tasting pudding served with roast beef and gravy.

Baked Ham

1 ham
Water

Place ham in roasting pan and add about 2 cups of water. Roast in oven at 350 degrees F for the time required depending size of ham. Can make ham gravy from the liquid if desired.

See Liquid Gravy Method recipe-

195

PRESERVING – CANNING – FREEZING – RENDERING

CANNING METHODS & PRESERVED FRUITS

Quote-
"Canning is an Art, and one in which every household member may excel, providing proper methods of procedure are followed. Fruits, Meats, Fowl and Vegetables are a part of our nation's food, and order that we may accomplish the very best in nutritional value".

General Canning Directions-
-Proper processing renders inactive all micro-organisms, such as yeast, bacteria and mold.

If you have failed to sterilize; that is, failed to destroy the micro-organism in the food, the seal will release. This will not be the fault of the jar or cap, but be due to the fact that you have not processed the food long enough to kill the micro-organisms. Follow reliable time tables carefully being sure temperature of canner is not too low or irregular during processing periods.

-Do not use jars which are cracked or nicked from previous use or which have sharp sealing edges.

-See that no seeds, food, or grease are lodged between lid and sealing surface of jar.

-In Oven Canning, set temperature at 250 degrees F. Start counting time when oven is turned on. Temperature should not exceed 250 degrees F. Do not allow jars to touch each other or sides of oven.

-If using wide mouth jars or narrow mason jars, see that screw band is turned down firmly tight BEFORE proceeding.

-In open kettle canning, filling only ONE STERILIZED JAR AT A TIME, with boiling hot product. Immediately wipe off top of jar and place scalded lid on jar with sealing composition next to glass and screw band firmly tight.

-When jars are packed with pre-cooked foods, place them in the canner for processing immediately. Do not allow them to stand.

-When jars of food are removed from the canner, set them out of a draft but far enough apart to allow the free circulation of air around them. Do not stack the jars. Do not cover with a cloth or place them back in boxes until the contents are cold.

-Do not pack jars tight with foods, such as Corn, Peas, Greens, Lima Beans and Meats. A tight pack prevents heat from properly penetrating to center of jar.

-Never open jars at end of processing to refill with liquid. Loss of liquid from the jar does not affect the keeping quality.

-If using pressure cooker, open long enough – 7 to 10 minutes – to expel all air from the cooker, otherwise pressure may not correspond to inside temperature.

-Be sure you thoroughly understand procedure in whatever method of canning you use.

-Jars such as mayonnaise or pickle jars should never be used for canning fruits, but may be used successfully for jams, jellies and pickles.

-The greatest possible care should be taken in removing tops from canned fruits, so that the glass is not injured. Punch a hole in all metal lids, and they will be easily removed.

-Never use a metal ring that is rusted, twisted or nicked in any way.

-Remember that proper sterilization is one of the most vital necessary rules of canning. Lack of it may result in any number of different things, causing failures. This does not mean just sterilizing the jar, but the fruit as well.

-For instance, peaches will very often turn brown if not properly sterilized, which means cooking them 3 minutes in the syrup before placing them in the jars for the hot water bath.

-Remember that hot syrups shrink the small fruits. For example, when doing raspberries, the jars should be filled 1/3 full with the syrup that has been allowed to cook. Then pack the berries into the syrup very closely. Seal and process by your favorite method.

-Berries or small fruit done in this way will never rise, and will not shrink. The fruits will also retain a very natural flavor.

Sterilized Jars

Wash jars in soapy hot water, hot enough to handle with your hands then rinse in clean hot water. Scalded and then turn upside down on a freshly sterilized cloth

Sterilized Glass Tops, Rubber Rings and Metal Rings

Wash the glass tops the same way as jars and then takes the rubber rings and metal rings separately and sterilize with hot water, scalded.

Sealing With Glass Lid, Rubber Ring and Metal Ring

When using glass jars for canning, they can be filled to almost overflow. Put sterilized rubber ring in place on glass top, place the glass top on jar opening and lastly the screw band over glass top, sealing tightly. After processing is completed, remove jars from hot water, tighten screw band if necessary, and turn jar upside down for testing of leakage. It is best to let jars remain in your kitchen for a day or so before storing, so that you may check them well to be sure that all jars are perfectly sealed.
.

Canning Methods

Cold Pack Method

Wash and prepare fruit as for serving, and pack raw in clean, hot jars. If fruit is to be peeled, dip into boiling water until the skins loosen and then into cold water. Slip skins off. Pack in jars and pour over hot syrup, leaving a space of one inch in top of metal-top jar, filling them full if glass-top jar is used. Paddle, that is, remove air bubbles by inserting the blade of a knife down the side of the jar, allowing liquid to circulate all through the jar. Adjust new scalded rubbers and tops. Seal. Place jars in preserving canner, fill with warm water to the tops of the jars. Bring to boil and process the required length of time.

Hot Pack Method

In the hot pack method, fruits are cooked for a short time on top of the stove in an open kettle, pre-cooked. This method shrinks the fruit and drives out the air bubbles. Pour pre-cooked fruits in the boiling syrup for 3 minutes. Pack at once as hot as possible into hot, scalded jars. Adjust new scalded rubbers and seal. Place jars in kettle containing 6 cups of hot water and process as usual.

Open Kettle Canning

This method, commonly used for canning fruits, requires greater skill than any other. It should never be used for canning low acid vegetables and meats. And is not as reliable as a hot water bath for canning fruits. If using, prepare and use jars, caps, lids and rubbers as instructed. Cook food thoroughly but not until mushy. Work at the stove so that everything can be kept boiling hot. The work must be done carefully, yet quickly. Fill and seal one jar at a time.

Caution in Open Kettle Method

In using the Open Kettle Method, there are several points well worth remembering. Long boiling of syrup results in a strong undesired flavor and the color is impaired. Consequently it is always best to divide the prepared syrup in two or three equal parts. Keep each division of syrup warm until required. The fruit should never be allowed to boil rapidly, but rather should barely simmer, care being taken never to crowd the fruit in an attempt to hurry it through. Just do as much fruit as the juice will cover. Keep the kettle securely covered during the cooking and finish off each kettle of fruit as it is ready.

Open Kettle Method

Wash and prepare fruit as for serving. Make syrup by boiling sugar and water together for 5 minutes. Add the fruit, let boil slowly according to length of time indicated. Test with a skewer or toothpick. Wash and sterilize jars and keep them in hot water until ready to fill. Remove from water by lifting jar with a wooden spoon. Set jar in a small pan, and fill jar at once to the top with boiling fruit and syrup. If metal top jars are used, fill within one inch of the top. Slip the blade of a knife around the inside of jar, to exclude all air and allow the syrup to circulate around the fruit. On the sterilized jar place a glass lid with a new scalded rubber ring and metal band and seal at once. The work of filling and sealing must be done rapidly and fruit must be boiling hot when put into jars to avoid introducing bacteria. Fill and seal each jar before proceeding to the other. Place the jars on a board with spaces between, to cool quickly. Keep out of draft. If glass top jars are used, tighten the bands gradually as the glass cools. Turn the jars upside down to test for leakage. Cook only a small quantity of fruit at a time to retain flavor and shape. If a large quantity of fruit is to be canned at one time it is best to make the required amount of syrup, then divide it into two kettles, keeping the second one on the back of the stove or over a low heat until required. This way the syrup does not become strong or dark with long cooking. Do not crowd the syrup with fruit. Fill and seal jar or two with finished fruit, cover with syrup and seal at once before proceeding with more.

Fruits Preserved Without Sugar

Fruits may be successfully canned without sugar by using boiling water instead of sugar-syrup. Fruits canned without sugar should be closely packed for best results. It must be noted however, that only the water bath method should be used. Do not use the open kettle method.

Fruit	Times for Processing (pints and quarts)
Peaches	25 minutes
Pears	35 minutes
Plums	25 minutes
Apples	35 minutes
Blueberries	25 minutes
Cherries	25 minutes

*fruits and berries preserved without sugar for pies and desserts and people who cannot have sugar.

Freezing

Quick Freeze

Quick-frozen foods offer a number of advantages that are not found in foods prepared by other methods of preservation. More food value is retained. The frozen product resembles fresh food in color, flavor and texture. Less time is required for preparing food for freezing. There is no danger of food poisoning while the goods are held in their frozen state. Fruits that are eaten raw may be held in their ripe state and served out of season.

For quick freezing, select fruits and vegetables at the proper degree of maturity for "good eating". Good quality meats and poultry are a necessity for satisfactory results. Freezing will not make poor products over into good ones, so quality is a must. Speed is essential in quick-freezing. Prepare and freeze products immediately after harvesting, handling small quantities at a time to avoid loss of color, flavor and appearance. Follow directions carefully for preparation, blanching and packaging. Put your packaged fruits and vegetables into the freezer right after being packaged

Frozen Vegetables

Practically all vegetables except those which are eaten raw as salad vegetables, namely lettuce, celery, radishes, cucumbers, tomatoes, cabbage and onions quick-freeze unsatisfactorily. Select young, tender vegetables of the proper variety. Prepare and wash as for canning. Vegetables for quick-freeze require a preliminary blanch. This is a MUST. Steam or boiling water for a specified length of time may be used for blanching.

Water Blanch

Place the prepared vegetables in boiling water for the length of time specified on a chart. (access chart for blanching instructions) Use a large covered container with a capacity of 6 to 10 quarts (24 cups to 40 cups). Put the vegetables in a strainer, which sits in the container. Blanch only one pound (2 cups) at a time.

Steam Blanch

Have water at a full rolling boil. Place the vegetables in a steamer, so that they are in a high steam, preparing just one pound (2 cups) at a time. Blanching time for vegetables begins when the water returns to boil, after the vegetables have been added. Use a high heat. Drain vegetables well and chill quickly to about 50 degrees F. Use an ample supply of ice water or cold running water. Keep the vegetables moving in the cold water, so that all parts are cooled. Left too long in the water, the vegetables may become waterlogged. If, however, they are not cooled completely they <u>will go sour</u>. Package and seal bags, place in freezer as soon as possible.

Garlic Dill Pickles

Brine-
16 cups water
2 cups vinegar
¾ cup pickling salt

Mix all ingredients together and bring to a boil and boil for 5 minutes, making sure that the salt is dissolved.

Cucumber & Dill Preparation-
Wash pickling cucumbers; rinse dill. Place a stem of fresh dill in each sterilized glass jar. Add one peeled clove of garlic; add cucumbers until the jar is full. Sprinkle 1 tsp. pickling spice on top. Pour hot brine over the cucumbers, filling the jar to the top. Place lid on and seal tightly. Turn jar up-side down and place on a cloth for 24 hours. Then re-tighten the lid and place jars in a cool storage area.

****

My family is a big fan of dill pickles. Each year the shelves in the basement were lined with at least 100 quart jars, and by time spring came, the shelves were empty.

Refrigerator Pickles

Brine-
4 cups white sugar
4 cups vinegar
1 ¾ tsps. celery seed
1 1/3 tsps. mustard seed
1 ½ tsps. turmeric
1/3 cup pickling salt

Mix ingredients in canner, bring brine to a boil, stirring until sugar and pickling salt is dissolved.

3 to 6 cups small white onions- peeled
12 cups cucumbers - sliced
1 medium size cauliflower - cut into bit size pieces - optional

Add onions, cucumbers and cauliflower to brine and stir. Let sit in canner for 24 hours. Place pickles in ice cream pails or jars making sure brine covers the mixtures. Cover with lid and place in the fridge. Will keep for several months

Mustard Pickles Chow Chows

2 heads cauliflower-cut into small pieces
8 cups cucumbers- sliced
8 cups onions- small white
4 cups beans- green
2 green peppers- chopped
6 cups vinegar
8 oz. mustard powder
3 tsps. Turmeric
3 – 4 cups brown sugar
1 cup flour
1 tbsp. celery seed

Prepare by cutting vegetables into bit size pieces except the onions. Stir 5 cups of vinegar and water together, bring to a boil making hot brine, pour over vegetables making sure they are covered with brine. Let stand overnight. Drain brine off vegetables and wash with cold water.

Mix mustard, flour, sugar, celery seed, and turmeric with a small amount of vinegar to make a smooth paste. Add to remaining cup of vinegar. Cook mustard mixture until thickened, stir in vegetables and cook about 20 minutes. Pour into sterilized glass jars and seal. Makes 8 jars.

Beet Pickles

Brine-
2 cups sugar
2 cups water
2 cups vinegar

Mix all ingredients together and bring to a boil and boil for 5 minutes, making sure that the sugar is dissolved. Let cool to almost tepid.

Beet Preparation-
Select approximately 8 cups small beets, cook until tender, dip in cold water and remove the skins. Pour brine over beets and simmer for 15 minutes, pack in sterilized glass jars and seal.

Bread & Butter Pickles

16 cups sliced cucumbers- do not peel
1 cup salt
4 ½ cups brown sugar
3 ½ cups vinegar
1 tsp. turmeric
4 cups sliced onions
10 ½ cups water
1 ½ cups water
½ tsp. celery seed

Use fresh cucumbers and medium sized onions. Slice onions and cucumbers and soak in brine overnight.

BRINE: 1 cup salt, 9 cups water. In the morning, drain off brine. Mix sugar, vinegar, 1 ½ cups water, and turmeric and celery seed together, add the drained onions and cucumbers and cover. Bring to boil and leave about 10 minutes, then put in sterilized jars and seal. Makes 9 jars.

Dilled Carrots

Brine-
16 cups water
2 cups vinegar
¾ cup pickling salt

Mix all ingredients together and bring to a boil and boil for 5 minutes, making sure that the salt is dissolved. Keep brine hot.

Carrot & Dill Preparation-
Wash small carrots, size of your finger; rinse dill. Place fresh picked dill in each sterilized glass jar. Add carrots, length wise in jar until full. Pour hot brine over the carrots, filling the jar to the top. Place lid on and seal tightly. Turn jar up-side down and place on a cloth for 24 hours. Then re-tighten the lid and place jars in a cool storage area.

****

Dilled carrots were a family favorite, and years later they are still a favorite of all, including my grandchildren.

Saskatoon Jam

Saskatoon berries
Sugar
Water

*¾ cups sugar to 1 cup of berries

Jams are made from crushed fruits cooked with sugar until the mixture is more or less homogeneous and thick. Well-ripened, yet sound berries and soft-fleshed fruits like Saskatoon's make good jam. The standard proportion of sugar varies from ¾ to 1 part by weight of sugar to 1 part by weight of the prepared fruit. After measuring the proportions of sugar, water and fruit, Heat slowly until the sugar is dissolve, stirring constantly. Continue stirring while cooking 10 to 15 minutes or until the thick jelly stage is reached. Pour into hot sterilized jars and seal.

Saskatoon's – Canned

Saskatoon berries
1 cup sugar
2 cups water

To make syrup, add sugar to water, bring to boil. Boil five minutes. (2 cups water and 1 cup sugar makes 2 ¼ cups medium syrup.)

Note: To determine the amount of syrup required, pack a quart jar with raw fruit, cover it completely with water. Pour the water off and measure it, then multiply it by the number of jars being used. This will let you know how many quarts of Saskatoon's you will need.

Preparing the Saskatoon's to be canned by filling a large bowl with cold water, about ¾ full and then fill the bowl with berries with just enough water so they float. Stir berries gently and hand pick out the berries that are not ripe, discolored, insect eaten or very small. Once the selected berries are clean, set aside.

Fill each jar ¾ full with the washed and dry berries.

Carefully pour the liquid syrup over the berries in the jar covering the berries at rim level.
Place rubber ring on glass top and glass top into metal screw top and place on each jar tightly.

Use a metal canner which will hold five quarts sealers, fill with lukewarm water, enough to cover the bottom of the canner estimated 3" deep. Place each jar into canner and cover with lid. Place on stove burner and cook for 1 hour and 8 minutes. Cooking process will be done once the time is completed. Carefully take out each jar, tighten the lid and turn up-side down on a cloth and let cool. Store in a cool area.

Saskatoon Picking

As a youngster going Saskatoon picking was like a picnic for the whole family. Everyone went, mom, dad, my sisters and brothers. We could be seen skipping and bouncing down a dusty trail in the middle of the field with our pails, usually old syrup tins, and of course, the prepared snacks – sandwiches and Kool-Aid.

Mom always picked a bright sunny day when the Saskatoon's were ready and in full fruit stage. They hung like big purple grapes, juicy and delicious. The thick Saskatoon bushes grew on the side of a small gully, along the south-east field.

Our intention was to fill up the large pails mom and dad carried, before we returned home. Everybody picked, no matter how old or big you were. The best way to pick the berries was to hook your pail handle to your belt or tie it around your waist with a rope or scarf. Some of us taller siblings pulled down the branches for the younger, shorter siblings to pick. We were always reminded not to break any of these branches, as the bush needed to grow for next year. And of course, we watched out for the bumble bees and hornets, which surprised us on occasion.

Once the big pails and our small pails were full, we gathered up everything and headed home, usually in time for mom to start supper.

Our task was not finished yet. Cleaning all those berries was next on the list. We poured the berries into a large pan of cold water, and then picked out the nice big round purple berries, leaving the half eaten by bugs, or shriveled or the wrong color berries to be thrown out. Once this was done, some of these berries were used for supper, in the form of a nice bowl of berries with sugar and cream, or a pie. The rest were to be canned, for our winter fruit. Rows and rows of glass mason jars filled with purple berries would be placed on the shelves in the cellar.

Dianne Saskatoon picking.

Strawberry Picking

My sisters, brothers and I would scout out the strawberry patch, which was along a grassy slough area on the west field, about a half mile from the house.

Picking wild strawberries was like finding precious red gems on the ground spread out over an area of covered greens. Some years, the berries would be thumb size and easier to pick. Other years, these tiny delicate berries were small, and took many hours of picking to make a dent in the pail.

Sometimes there would be enough strawberries, to pick for jam, but most times it was only an outing for the kids to pick some strawberries and have that picnic.

This was kid's time, a time to play, pick some berries, have a picnic, and not eat the strawberries. If we did bring any strawberries home, mom would make a dessert from our small contribution of berries for supper.

Most times the strawberry jam was made with a mix of other fruits.

My sister Lorraine mentioned that, as kids if we went out to pick wild strawberries in our favorite strawberry patch, we had to sneak away from the house, and not let our old dog Bugs know we had left. Apparently, this old dog liked strawberries, and would eat all the berries.

Wild Strawberries

Once the berries are cleaned, after taking out the leaves, tiny twigs and not so ripe berries, the strawberries where ready to eat, a nice bowl of berries with sugar and cream.

3-Minute Strawberry Jam

4 cups strawberries - slices
4 cups sugar
½ lemons thinly sliced

Combine sliced berries, sugar and sliced lemon. Place over low heat until sugar is dissolved. Increase heat and bring to full rolling boil. Boil hard for exactly 8 minutes. Allow to stand for 1 minute, remove any scum, and pour into sterilized jars and seal.

Raspberry Jam

1 lb. raspberries
2/3 cups sugar
½ of lemon - juice

Combine raspberries and sugar, place over heat, bring to a boil. Boil very rapidly about 20 minutes, stir constantly. Add lemon juice and boil until it jellies, about 5 to 10 minutes longer.

Raspberries - Canned

Syrup-
1 cup sugar
2 cups water

Boil together for 5 minutes. Fill sterilized jars half full of raspberries. Pour boiling syrup over fruit and seal jars tightly. Have ready a large preserving canner with a lid. Fill container about 4 inches of boiling water in the bottom. Set the jars in the water. Fill the canner with boiling water half way to the top of the jars. Cover with lid and allow the jars to stand in canner until water is cool. Make sure the jars are sealed. Store in a cool dark place.

Wild Raspberries

Raspberry picking was also a family outing. There were no wild raspberries on the family farm land, so the family was loaded up in the car, with all sizes of syrup and lard pails, and off we went to a well-known raspberry spot. By this time there were seven kids.

The best places to find wild raspberry bushes weren't always along the roadsides, but in old gravel pits. We picked raspberries north of highway #2, not too far from Odette's farm, a family our parent knew.

Lots of raspberry bushes flourished in this old gravel pit, and along the gravel road. Good thing there was limited traffic so the berries weren't dusty. Dad would park the car, and we would inspect all the bushes, and then select one that looked like it had the most berries. We would start picking berries, trying not to get pricked by the thorns on the bushes, and being careful not to get stung by the bees buzzing nearby. While we were picking berries in midafternoon there was lots of laughing and conversation. Once again, we were warned not to break any branches or stomp down any bushes. After filling our pails, we would go back home, and quickly clean the berries, so we could have a big bowl of berries with cream and sugar. Yummy!

In my later years, berry picking meant scouting for a good patch of berries, not too far from home, and enough berries to make my time worthwhile. No planned picnic time. I would encourage my young children to help pick berries, but wasn't always successful.

My raspberry canning experiences were not always as successful as I hoped. My intent was to pick berries and canned them for winter, hoping everyone would enjoy the fruit, and maybe help mom next year.

I'm not too sure what or how, but every year I managed to make raspberry fruit that didn't process right. Followed the directions from my mom's recipe to the exact measurements, but instead the fruit fermented. I couldn't use any of this fruit for eating purposes; but I did find another way for my fruit to be enjoyed or consumed.

Jim's dad, Bob, was famous at making wine, and guess what; he made use of my canned raspberries! Yes, raspberry wine! I would have never thought of it, but he did, and I was never without a bottle of raspberry wine or two.

SUGAR SYRUP TABLE

For Canning Fruits

Very Light   1 cup sugar/4 cups water----------makes 4 ½ cups syrup

Light   1 cup sugar/3 cups water----------makes 3 ½ cups syrup

Medium   1 cups sugar/2cups water----------makes 2 ¼ cups syrup

Heavy   1 cup sugar/1 cup water -----------makes 1 ½ cups syrup

To make syrup, add sugar to water, bring to boil. Boil five minutes.

NOTE-
To determine the amount of syrup required, pack a quart jar with raw fruit, cover it completely with water. Then pour the water off and measure it, then multiply it by the number of jars of fruit to be made.

Combining Sugar & Juice-

In order to have the best possible product, work with small lots of juice at a time, not more than 8 cups. Measure the sugar and the juice accurately. Use ¾ to 1 cup of sugar to each cup of juice. Use a good grade of granulated white sugar.

Pear Jam

4 lbs. pear peelings
3 lbs. sugar
¾ cup water
1 tsp. nutmeg
1 tbsp. cinnamon

Cook pear peeling on medium heat until all peelings are tender. May need to add a small amount of water. Put peeling through a sieve, turning the peelings into a thick liquid. Place pear liquid in a sauce pan, add sugar and spices and bring to a boil, stirring constantly. Once the liquid forms into a thick jelly stage, pour into sterilized jars and seal.

Basic Jam

Wash and stem the fruit (place in a colander and hold under cold water tap, then drain well) Crush some of the fruit slightly to create a little bit of water to start the boil. Simmer for 5 minutes; add the sugar (3/4 lb. sugar for each pound of fruit). Stir well, bring to quick boil and boil hard until thick and clear. The time varies according to the fruits; therefore they must be watched very closely the last few minutes of boiling. Use a good-sized kettle to allow for a full rolling boil. The quicker the jam is boiled, the less pectin is lost. Stir often to avoid burning during the last few minutes. Remove from heat; allow to stand a moment or two for scum to rise and set, so it can be skimmed off easily. Place in jars, seal and cool before placing in storage.

Canning Fresh Fruit

Pear

Peel, cut in halves, and core. Pack the pears into sterilized jars and fill with medium syrup, seal, and ready for canning for 1 hour and 15 minutes in canner, placed on top of stove on medium heat.

See Syrup chart-

Plum

Plums are ordinarily canned whole, and they should be gathered just as they are beginning to ripen. After they are washed, prick each plum with a fork to prevent the skin from bursting. Pack into jars and cover with hot medium syrup. Seal and place into canner for canning for 1 hour and 8 minutes on top of stove on medium heat.

See Syrup chart-

Peach

To prepare peaches for canning, immerse them in boiling water for about ½ minute or until the skins will slip off easily. Plunge at once into cold water for a few seconds, remove the skins, cut the peaches into halves, and discard the pits. Pack raw peaches in jars; fill jars with hot syrup (light or medium syrup). Place in canner for canning for 1 hour and 8 minutes on top of stove on medium heat.

See Syrup chart-

****

When canning season hit on the farm, it was like a marathon. Cases of different kinds of fruit were bought at the grocery store in town. A lot of the times the fruit was not quite ripe, but, when the timing was just right, the canning jars were brought up from the cellar, washed, sterilized and ready for the fruit. Peaches, Pears and Plums were the most common fruit mom canned. The finished product was proudly lined up on the cupboard to cool before storing.

In the later years, I followed mom's tradition of canning fruit for the winter. I also made jams yearly, trying out many different varieties.

Mom continued to can even after her children left home. Guess this habit was a way of insuring food was preserved for winter time. She felt a real sense of great accomplishment of seeing the enjoyment her family members would have when enjoying a good feed of fruit, and/or desserts made from the canned fruit.

Stewed Tomatoes – canned

3 cups celery - chopped
1 cup onions - chopped
3 green peppers -chopped
2 tsps. salt
1 tsp. pepper
5 cups tomatoes - diced
1 – 48 oz. can tomato juice

Mix all ingredients together and cook in a heavy pan until vegetables are tender. Pour into sterilized jars and seal.

Sandwich Spread

6 cucumbers
1 red pepper
2 onions
1 green pepper
¼ cup salt
Vinegar

Put cucumbers, onions and peppers through a food chopper, sprinkle with ¼ cup salt, let stand overnight. Drain well. Cover with vinegar, bring to a boil, and then add the following ingredients.

¾ cup sugar
2 eggs- beaten
1 tsp. dry mustard
1 tbsp. flour
½ cup thick sour cream
¼ cup margarine
1 tsp. celery seed

Continue to stir, pour into sterilized jars and seal at once.
Makes 3 jars

Antipasto

Chopping all the vegetables first. This will take about 2 hours, a blender shouldn't be used.

Cook the following, stirring constantly for 10 minutes.

8 oz. olive oil
1 very large cauliflower -cut bite size pieces
2 tins of black olives - chopped
1 – 16 oz. tin broken green olives
2 – 12 oz. jars pickled onions – chopped

Then add -
2 – 10 oz. tins mushrooms - stems & pieces
2 – large green peppers -chopped
2 – 4 oz. tins pimentos -chopped
4 – 15 oz. Heinz catsup
1 – 15 oz. Heinz hot catsup
1 – 48 oz. jar mixed pickles - chopped

Simmer another 10 minutes stirring often.

Drain and pour boiling water over the following to rinse.
2 - tins anchovies –chopped
3 - 7 oz. tins of solid tuna – chopped
1 - tin small shrimp

Add anchovies, tuna and shrimp to the mixture, stir and place in sterilized jars and process in a canner for 10 minutes to seal.

Jean Hogg

NOTE-
In the 70's, this cost was about $50.00 to make and made about 20 pints.
Jean told me this is fun to make with someone, and a few bottles of wine makes it seem to go even faster!

Canning Moose Meat

After the moose has been skinned, butchered and quartered, the meat is then ready to be canned or cut into family size packages and froze.

From the hind quarter cut the meat, into 2" x 2" cubes. Place into mason quart jars filling to the top. Add salt and pepper and pour water over meat up to rim of jar. Place a rubber ring on to a glass top and glass top into metal screw top and place on each jar tightly. Place into canner.
Use a metal canner which holds five quart sealers. Fill with lukewarm water, enough to cover the bottom of the canner estimated 3 to 5 inches deep. Place the jars into canner and place lid on canner. Put on stove burner and boil for 1 ½ to 2 hours. Cooking process will be done once the time is complete. Carefully take out each jar, tighten the lid and place on a cloth and let cool. Meat should be jellied once cooled. Store in cool storage area

****

Jim's mum taught me the skill of preparing moose meat for canning. When she first arrived on the farm she didn't know anything about canning wild meat, nor had she ever seen such an animal much less eaten it. However, there was an elderly lady who lived not far from her, taught her the same skills she taught me.

Spending a day in my mother-in-law's kitchen, cutting meat in preparation of canning was one lesson that has stayed with me for a long time. After learning the technique, I proudly went home to can moose meat, every year for my family. Of course this depended on my great hunter, and whether he succeeded in getting his moose that year or not.

Jim often took a jar of moose meat and a loaf of bread with him on his mechanic service trips, which often took him into unknown roads many miles away. He called it his "jungle lunch", because he didn't know if he would be back for supper or the next day. I guess this was part of his survival kit.

"Jungle Lunch?" I'm not really sure where the expression came from. Maybe it resembled the long road trips into the unknown, driving down a cut line or a deserted road lined on both sides with thick bush, and no sign of any activity. A road going no where!

****

Being raised in a family who never ate wild meat, except when a relative would bring the family a piece of meat. I was unfamiliar how to butcher, prepare, cook or even can wild meat.

Then! Marry into a family who hunt regularly, every season, and bringing home their prize, which could be a moose, deer, geese or ducks, you soon learn how to prepare these meats for meals. I actually became quite good in these skills I might say.

Wild Game Marinade

1 bottle dry red wine
½ cup red or white vinegar
2 carrots – sliced
3 onions- sliced
½ tsp. whole black peppercorns or ½ tsp. black pepper
½ tsp. cloves
½ tsp. juniper berries – optional
½ tsp. thyme
1 tbsp. salt
3 tbsps. parsley – dried
1 bay leaf

Trim fat off meat, cut into pieces and place in a glass or enamel bowel. Combine ingredients, mix well and pour over meat. Cover. Refrigerate for 24 hours for smaller cuts of meat, and longer for the larger cuts. Turn the meat several times if the marinate does not cover the meat. Remove the meat when ready, pat dry and cook.

Jerky

4 pounds of game meat cut into 1" x 2" x 8" strips
2 tsps. salt
2 tsps. powdered barbeque seasoning
2 tsps. chili pepper
2 tsps. curry powder

Cut all fat, gristle and tendons from strips of meat. Combine all the seasonings in a salt shaker. Sprinkle the meat with the seasoning and pound into the meat strips. Scatter the remaining seasoning mixture across the top side of each strip of meat. Place the seasoning strips on an oven rack at 150 degrees F. The strips should be left for 7 hours or until most of the moisture is receded from the meat. When finished, the strips should be dry like leather but supple enough to bend without breaking.

Hunting Excursion

My hubby went goose hunting every season, so I thought I would like to go along and enjoy an outing.

As you have read, my family didn't hunt, so I thought this would be an opportunity to learn something new. I also didn't know much about guns.

So, one fall afternoon, I went with Jim and his buddy to spot geese, which were in a field not far from our home. We walked into the field, found a spot to settle, squatted and waited for the geese to fly. Prior to leaving the house, Jim had given me some instructions on how to hold a shot gun, aim and shoot.

We quietly waited for the geese to fly, and then all of a sudden a goose flew up and Jim yelled shoot! I aimed and pulled the trigger. I didn't know how a jolt on my shoulder could off-set my balance. The next thing I knew, I was ass over tea kettle, on my back side, still holding the gun and my shoulder hurt.

The joke was on me. The goose was too far away and of course I missed!

This was my first and last time I wanted to go hunting with the guys. I thought it best to stay home and wait for the hunter to bring the bird's home. Not recommended if you just want an afternoon outing, I am sure there are other more exciting ventures to participate in.

Sauerkraut Stuffed Duck

¾ cup chopped onions
½ cup chopped celery
2 apples –diced
¼ cup butter
4 cups sauerkraut – drained
1 average size duck
2 strips of bacon

Prepare duck for roasting, soaking in a baking soda solution for one hour. Rinse and drain well. Sprinkle salt inside and outside of duck. Rub with butter. Sauté ½ cup of butter, onions, celery until lightly browned. Add drained sauerkraut and apple to the onion and celery mixture and blend well. Fill cavity of duck. Place strips of bacon over the duck, cover and bake at 350 degrees F for 2 hours.

Roast Goose with Potato Stuffing

1 wild goose - 8 to 10 lbs.
1 tsp. salt
½ tsp. pepper

Clean the goose thoroughly and pat dry. Rub cavity and outside with salt and pepper mixture.

Stuffing Mixture-
8 to 10 medium size potatoes -boiled
2 tbsps. butter
1 cup onions- chopped
½ cup celery -chopped
4 slices bread -crumbled
¼ lb. ground bacon
2 eggs - beaten
1 tsp. poultry seasoning
1 tsp. salt
½ tsp. pepper
½ tsp. garlic powder

Boil the potatoes, drain and mash or rice the potatoes. (Save the potato water for basting the goose.) Melt butter in a skillet and sauté onions and celery, DO NOT brown. Add to riced potatoes, bread crumbs, bacon, eggs, poultry seasoning, salt, pepper and garlic powder. Stuff goose with mixture. Roast in covered roaster for 4 hours at 325 degrees F. Continue basting with potato water until done.

****

My best results when cooking a goose, duck or wild meat occurred; when I used my father-in-law's homemade choke cherry wine or raspberry wine. This made the meat tender, and took the wild taste out.

Note- After half hour of roasting of the bird or roast, pour two cups of wine over the meat and continue to baste until done.

230

Smoked Fish

All fish should be kept cool prior to being placed in a smoker, in order to preserve the firmness. In order to reduce shrinkage, the skin may be left on the fillets if desired. If the fish pieces are cut to 1" thickness, they will cook more evenly in the smoker. Fish do not have to be de-boned for smoking because the meat will flake away from the bone easily after cooking.

Marinade – Brine for Fish

2 pounds of fish

Brine-
8 cups water
1 cup coarse pickling salt
½ cup brown sugar
1 ½ ozs. Lemon juice
1 tsp. garlic salt
4 slices of onion

Stir mixture together until well dissolved, stir in onions.
Soak fish – 1 hour.

Fish Story

This is one of these particular summer days that we travelled north, to an area where my grandparents, Steve and Annie Wurst's, old homestead was located, along the Whitemud river.

The river was low that year and it was a perfect sunny day, for the kids to wade and splash around in the water and a fishing day with our friends. We chose a spot, and walked down to the river, so the kids could play.

The guys decided to go further upstream where the water was deeper, to do some fishing, for our fish fry that evening. Apparently the fish were visible in the clear water, but weren't biting. One crafty fish kept swimming around the hook several times, refusing to take the bait, just kept swimming around and around.

Well! Someone had a bright idea how to make this fish become part of the planned fish fry. This individual made a quick decision, that he was going to use his pistol (which he brought along for protection of bears or other animals) to get that fish. Yes! He shot the fish! This is not a whopper of a fish story, but actually happened. And we did have a fish fry that evening.

Rendering Pork Lard

Preparing to render lard is a lengthily process. First cut the fat off of the pork meat found in the areas when trimming the pork chops and hind quarter area. Once the fat is trimmed off, cut into small size pieces or strips and place into a heavy pot (good quality weight which will not burn) and fill almost to the top. Turn stove burner on low to medium heat. Slowly the fat will heat up and begin to melt. Stir often and make sure the fat does not brown or burn. Once the fat has completely melted, let it cool to lukewarm, and then pour into sterilized mason jars and seal. Place in a cool storage area for later use.

Baked Piggy Puffs

Piggy puffs as we called them, were made from the rind (outer skin of the pig). The process is to slice off the fat of the skin and around the fatter parts of the meat which was used for rendering of lard. The rind or outer skin was then cut into small chunks and placed on a cookie sheet. Place in the oven at 300 degrees F and bake for one hour, turning the rind occasionally until it curls and puffs up. Keep watch on the rinds so they do not burn. Once cooked, sprinkle with salt. Ready to eat.

My fishing and hunting fella's – Jim, Robert and Stephen

234

My Pig Venture

My experience in raising pigs was very limited, even though my dad raised pigs on the farm.

Once we were settled on the acreage, Jim thought we should raise a pig or two, for our own use. Jim had the experience as his dad raised pigs, and he had helped with the feeding and watering.

A decision was made, but we needed a building. Unknown to me, Jim and our dear neighbor had discussed this issue and there was an old granary, which could be towed to our acreage, to be used as a shelter for the pig.

Well, the day came when this old rickety dilapidated wooden building was towed down the gravel road to our acreage. I wasn't sure if this building would make the trip, as it looked very unstable and you could see through it, because boards were missing on the walls. The granary was positioned just below the house, on the north east side along the tree line, parallel to the driveway. It provided quite a contrast to a new house.

Once the building was in place and an electric wire fence was set up, Jim went to buy a pig or two, from a farmer, who lived north of us.

To my surprise, Jim brings home not one or two pigs, but a big old mother pig and 10 piglets. Now we have eleven pigs. Yes, eleven pigs! I was not impressed, because I knew who would be monitoring these critters. And I was not convinced that an electric fence would keep anything confined, much less pigs. Of course, that year, the summer was hot and dry.

My major concern was my garden, which was a few hundred feet from this old granary and I knew if these pigs got out, I would be without a garden, as pigs root up everything.

The kids thought this was great; however, there were a few chores now.

These pigs did not stay in the fence, they wondered around the yard and the country side. It was frustrating, to go searching the neighborhood, looking for your pigs. Sometimes we found them in our garage resting or rooting up my new flower beds next to the house.

I hoped these critters would grow up fast and be ready for butchering soon. In the middle of pig monitoring, hubby goes fishing!!

After a few excursions looking for these pigs, Jim did put up a real fence and I was hoping this would hold them in, as these pigs were getting much bigger.

My experiences continued, throughout that hot summer. Even though the pigs had shade, they sun burnt. I certainly hadn't heard of this and now I was about to gained another experience, learning how to treat pigs with a sun burn!

The farmer's wife, from where Jim bought these pigs came to help treat our sun burnt pigs. She arrived with a liquid solution and a big metal container. What is the treatment? A liquid solution was mixed and poured into a large container of water, ready to dip each pig in. Now, we are not talking about little piglets, but pigs that are wiener size – over 40 pounds.

It was quite an experience for me, trying to catch a pig, dip the pig into the solution and then let go of it. Can you imagine two women chasing around a rooted up, mucky, dirt pig pen and catching squealing pigs? This had to be team work because it took both of us to grab a wiggly, squealing pig.

This all happened when the kids were at school, and hubby was at work.

Thank goodness, these critters became market size. When they were ready for butchering, I did my happy dance!

This part of taking the kid off of the farm, but not out of them, well that's not me! I didn't want to see another pig on the acreage ever again and everybody knew it. However, we did enjoy the hams, bacon and piggy puffs!!!!

FESTIVE SEASONS

Christmas Cheese Ball

4 cups shredded cheddar cheese
6 ozs. cream cheese
½ cup miracle whip
2 tsps. sherry flavoring – optional
1 tsp. Worcestershire sauce
1/8 tsp. onion salt
1/8 tsp. garlic salt
1/8 tsp. celery salt
½ cup chopped olives – green
½ cup dried beef chips-optional
½ tbsp. dried parsley – optional
½ cup chopped almonds – optional
*can use one of the options to decorate if desired

Mix together until creamy. Form into a ball. Roll in beef chips or parsley or almonds or decorate with olives slices. Wrap in saran wrap and refrigerate.

****

Once the children had their first taste of my cheese balls, it became a must in our home, especially for the holiday season. When the children became adults and left home, I now make a cheese ball for each family at Christmas time. Who would have thought that testing out a recipe would become a yearly tradition? I guess this is how many traditions begin.

Whipped Shortbread Cookies

1 lb. of butter- room temp
1 cup icing sugar
½ cup cornstarch
1 tsp. vanilla
3 cups flour

Blend butter, icing sugar, vanilla and cornstarch until smooth, add flour ½ cup at a time blending well between each addition. Spoon on to cookie sheet, place ½ maraschino cherry in center. Bake at 350 degrees F for approximately 10 to 15 minutes.

Merry Christmas!

Marjorie Wurst's Christmas Cake

3 cups raisins
4 cups chopped mixed peel
1 ½ cups glazed cherries cut in halves
2 cups sliced almonds
1 lemon – grated rind and juice of lemon
4 ½ cups flour
½ tsp. salt
1 tsp. baking powder
2 cups butter or margarine
2 cups sugar
9 eggs

In a separate bowl, combine fruits, nuts and lemon rind; dust with a little of the flour. Stir flour, salt, baking powder together in a separate bowl. In another bowl Cream butter or margarine until creamy and light; add sugar gradually beating between sugar additions. Add eggs one at a time, beating well after each one. (If mixture curdles add a little of the dry ingredients, then continue to add eggs) Blend in dry ingredients, mix well, fold in lemon juice, fruits and nuts and stir until the batter is completely mixed. Use three 9" x 5" loaf pans. Cut heavy waxed paper or brown butcher paper to fit each loaf pan. Grease the paper then place into each loaf pan. Pour in the batter filling the loaf pan ¾ full. Bake in slow oven at 275 degrees F for 3 ½ hours depending on size of pan or until done. Place a shallow pan of water on the bottom rack of oven during the baking time; remove the last hour of baking. Insert knife into middle of cake. If the knife comes out clean the cake is done. When cake is done, place on a rack to cool, before removing from the paper lining. Once cooled, remove paper and store in an air tight canister and place in a cool place.

****

Betty Ireland's well-seasoned Christmas Cakes

November was the time to start making Christmas cakes. Once the cakes were made they were kept enclosed in containers in cool storage in the cellar. Then, once a week Betty would go down to the cellar and pour a small portion of brandy over each cake. She nurtured her Christmas cakes until Christmas day, not letting anyone have a sample. We never knew how much brandy went into these cakes; we only knew they were wonderfully moist and delicious. I am sure there was a secret method to this, but I never did find out and nobody shared this information.

Cherry Almond Bundt Cake

2 cups red candied cherries – halved
½ cup sliced almonds
½ cup flour
1 cup margarine
1 cup sugar
1 tsp. vanilla
1 tsp. almond extract
4 eggs
1 ½ cups flour
2 tsps. baking powder
½ tsp. salt
1/3 cup milk

Combine cherries, almonds and ½ cup flour in a bowl. Mix until fruit is well coated set aside. Cream margarine, sugar and flavoring together until light and fluffy. Add eggs one at a time, beating for one minute on high speed of electric mixer after each addition. Combine 1 ½ cups flour, baking powder and salt. Stir well to blend. Add dry ingredients to creamed mixture alternately with milk, starting and ending with dry ingredients. Stir in floured fruits and nuts. Spread batter into greased and floured Bundt or tube pan. Bake at 300 degrees F for 55 to 65 minutes or until toothpick inserted in center comes out clean. Cool cake in pan 10 minutes, and then turn out onto wire rack to cool completely. Wrap cooled cake in aluminum foil and store in cool place for several days to allow cake to ripen.
Makes one cake.

Unbaked Brazil Nut Cake

3 cups Brazil nuts
1 ½ cups seedless raisins
½ lb. dates
½ lb. cherries
1 tbsp. orange rind – grated
¼ tsp. cinnamon
¼ tsp. nutmeg
¼ tsp. cloves
½ tsp. allspice
½ tsp. ginger
4 ½ cups graham wafers- crushed
½ lb. dates- cut-up
1 cup candied fruit- diced
1 lb. marshmallows
¾ cup orange juice
1 tsp. vanilla

Line 2 loaf pans with double thickness of waxed paper extending paper over the rim 3". Place whole nuts in a large mixing bowl; add graham wafers crumbs and the fruit. Cut marshmallows into double boiler; add orange juice, rind and spices. Heats until marshmallows are melted, stirring constantly. Add to fruit mixture, add vanilla and mix well together. Fill pans and press down well with a spoon. Fold wax paper over cakes. Store in refrigerator for several weeks.

Christmas Steamed Carrot Pudding

1 cup margarine
1 cup brown sugar
1 cup carrots – grated
1 cup potatoes – grated
1 cup raisins
1 cup currants
1 egg
1 tsp. salt
1 tsp. baking soda
1 tbsp. lemon
½ cup flour
½ tsp. cinnamon
½ tsp. cloves
½ tsp. nutmeg
2 tbsps. sour milk

Mix ingredients together until batter is drop texture. Fill glass quart jar ½ full and place glass top and ring on jar and tighten. Fill canner with 4 cups water. Place jars into canner on top of stove and let cook for 2 ½ hours. When cooked the pudding should have risen to almost fill the jars.
Take out of the canner, let cool. Makes 6 quarts.
*the pudding can be stored in a cool place until ready for Christmas dinner.

****

In the early years on the farm, Christmas Pudding was prepared and baked in a syrup can. The batter was poured into the tin and the lid place on tightly. Then the tin was placed in a shallow pan filled with about 2 inches of water. The pudding was baked in the wood cook stove oven. Many years later mom began putting the pudding into glass mason jars and cooked in a canner for 2 ½ hours.

Butter Scotch Sauce for Christmas Pudding

2 cups water
2 tbsps. cornstarch
2 tbsps. cold water
1 tsp. vanilla
½ cup brown sugar

Bring water to boiling point and turn heat down to medium. Add brown sugar. Mix cornstarch and cold water together until cornstarch is dissolved. Add to the hot water and brown sugar and mix until thickened, continue to stir until there are no lumps. Add vanilla, stirring until the sauce is well mixed and ready to be served.
Serve over Christmas Steamed Pudding warm.

****

At every Christmas dinner, mom served our favorite and traditional dessert. The Christmas Pudding was dished up and topped with butter scotch sauce. This tradition which started since 1948, or maybe even before, has been carried on within my family. My sisters have also carried this tradition on in their families.

Chocolates

Centers-
3 lbs. icing sugar
1 cup eagle brand milk
½ cup margarine
3 tbsps. white corn syrup

Mix together by hand until smooth, divide batter into equal amounts. Select flavorings – vanilla; strawberry, peppermint; almond; rum or any other favoring of choice. Add a different flavoring to each divided batter and work flavor into batter until well mixed. Form into balls or shapes of choice – round, square, balls etc. Chill in fridge for approximately 1 hour.

Coating-
1 box semi-sweet dark chocolate
1 box sweetened dark chocolate
½ bar paraffin wax

Melt the three ingredients using a double boiler pan; melting ingredients until a liquid form. Dip each center – ball, round, square and other shapes chosen into the chocolate until completely covered.

*after the shape or form is dipped can roll into fine coconut or chopped fine nuts.
*can use white chocolate instead of dark or milk chocolate.

Place each individual chocolate on a cookie sheet and place in fridge to cool. To store place in cool storage or in the freezer.
Ready for Christmas!

****

For a number of years, just before Christmas, I would make large batches of different flavored and shaped Christmas Chocolates. The family certainly enjoyed them, and as always, they didn't last very long

Golden Santa Bread

4 to 4 ½ cups flour
½ cup sugar
2 pkg. yeast
1 ½ tsps. salt
½ cup milk
¼ cup water
¼ cup butter
2 eggs
2 raisins
2 egg yolks
2 to 3 drops red food coloring

In a large mixing bowl, combine 2 cups flour, sugar, yeast and salt in a small sauce pan, heat the milk, water and butter to 120 degrees F. Add to dry ingredients; beat just until moistened. Beat in the eggs until smooth. Stir in enough remaining flour to form stiff dough. Turn onto a floured surface; knead until smooth and elastic, about 6 to 8 minutes. Place in a grease bowl turning once to grease top. Cover and let rise in a warm place until double about 1 hour. Punch dough down. Turn onto a lightly floured surface; divide into two portions, one slightly larger than the other. Shape the larger portion into an elongated triangle with roughed corners for Santa's head and hat. Divide the smaller portion in half. Shape and flatten one half into a beard. Using scissors or a pizza cutter, cut into strips to within 1" of top. Position on Santa's face, twist and curl strips if desired. Use the remaining dough for the mustache, nose, hat pom-pom and brim. Shape a portion of dough into a mustache, flatten and cut the ends into small strips with scissors. Place above beard. Place a small ball above mustache for nose. Fold tip of hat over and add another ball for pom-pom. Roll out a narrow piece of dough to create a hat brim, position under hat. With a scissors, cut two slits for eyes, insert raisins into slits. In separate small bowls, beat each egg yolk. Add red food coloring to one yolk, carefully brush over hat, nose and cheeks. Brush plain yolk over remaining dough. Cover loosely with foil. Bake at 350 degrees F for 15 minutes. Uncover; bake 10 – 12 minutes longer or until golden brown. Cool on a wire rack - Yields 1 loaf.

Taste of Home
Christmas Country Style Magazine
December 14, 2009

Shaping Santa

FIG. 1: On a lightly floured surface, shape the larger portion of bread dough into an elongated triangle with rounded corners for Santa's head and hat.

FIG. 2: Shape and flatten half of the smaller portion of dough into a beard. Using a scissors or pizza cutter, cut the beard into strips to within 1 in. of the top of the beard.

FIG. 3: Carefully pick up the cut beard piece with both hands and position the beard on the bottom of Santa's face.

FIG. 4: If desired, twist the cut strips in the beard and slightly curl up the ends of the strips to shape the beard.

FIG. 5: Add red food coloring to one beaten egg yolk and carefully brush the tinted red yolk over the hat, nose and cheeks.

Chocolate Confetti

¼ cup butter
½ cup peanut butter
1 pkg. semi-sweet chocolate chips
1 bag miniature marshmallows

Melt butter with peanut butter in a large sauce pan. Stir in chocolate chips until melted. Cool to warm temperature. Add marshmallows and stir until all coated. Line pan with wax paper, fold in mixture. Cool in refrigerator, cut into 36 pieces and freeze.

Variations- add ½ cup chopped walnuts or ½ cup medium coconut.

Easter Eggs –Home Made

1 cup eagle brand milk
1 tsp. almond extract
4 ½ cups coconut – fine unsweetened
4 ozs. ground almonds
2 pkgs. flavored gelatin – strawberry, orange or any favorite

Blend milk, almond extract, coconut and ground almonds in a bowl. Place mixture into two different bowls. Add 3 oz. flavored gelatin to each batch. Blend well. Chill. Roll into medium size Easter egg sizes. Makes 4 dozen of different flavors.

Chocolates

Filling-
¼ cup hot mashed potatoes
1 tsp. milk and butter
2 cups icing sugar
½ tsp. salt
Flavor of choice

Mix together until well mixed, then add flavoring. Melt chocolate, in a double boiler pan, until a liquid forms. Coat each center with melted chocolate – dark or white until completely covered.
Cool and store in cool storage.

Creamy Chocolate Truffles

3 pkgs. (175g each) semi-sweet chocolate chips
1 can eagle brand sweetened condensed milk
1 tbsp. (15ml) vanilla
*Coatings – flaked coconut or finely chopped nuts or unsweetened cocoa powder, icing sugar or chocolate sprinkles or other colored sprinkles

In heavy saucepan, over low heat melt chips with eagle brand milk. Remove from heat. Stir in vanilla. Chill for 2 hours or until firm enough to shape into 1" balls. Roll in any of the coatings. Chill for 1 hour. Store covered at room temperature.
Makes about 6 dozen truffles.

*Option- Creamy Chocolate Rum Truffles
Omit vanilla, stir in ¼ cup dark rum and ½ tsp. rum extract into melted chocolate mixture. Chill, shape and roll in flaked coconut.

Christmas Candy House
Every Child's Favorite

1 Card board – 24" x 24"
1 Tissue box – square shape
Foil
Scissors
Pencil
Tape
Ruler
Seven minute frosting
Candies – assorted

Cut card board into a 24" by 24" and cover completely with foil. Take a Kleenex box, a square shaped size, using as the main part of the house, then form a piece of thin cardboard into a roof shape and tape to the house. Place on covered foil cardboard and tape down so the house does not move.

Make the seven minute frosting, which will be soft, whipped and easy to manage when covering the house. Once the icing is spread over the house let it set for a bit, long enough so the icing becomes tacky. Now ice sickles can be formed on the edges of the roof if desired. Add candies to decorate the Christmas Candy House, to any design that will make treasured memories of spending time with the children.

See Seven Minute Frosting recipe-

****

Every Christmas season, I would make a Christmas Candy House with the children's help decorating. This was one of our holiday activities, while we were waiting for the special day to arrive.

CHRISTMAS!

Christmas Candy Wreath

1 wire clothes hanger
Ribbon- assorted colors
Assorted candies – wrapped
1 ribbon bow
Scissor's'
Measuring tape

Take a wire clothes hanger and form it into a circle, leaving the hooked end in original shape. Cut ribbon into 6" pieces. Tie a knot with 6" pieces of ribbon on one end of each wrapped candy and then tie onto the wire hanger. Continue to tie each candy on the wire until completely filled. Each candy should be pressed tightly together and once all the candies are tied onto the wire, take the ends of the ribbons and pull them forward, so the ribbons are tucked around the front of each candy, then curl the ends giving a curled design. Add a ribbon bow on the bottom of the wreath. Ready to display.

****

I made a Christmas Candy Wreath in red and gold colors, using candy wrapped in gold foil and tied with red ribbon. The Christmas Candy Wreath looked very attractive and fun for the children to sample the candies, once the Christmas season had ended.

SPECIAL SOUP

Cabbage Soup Diet
7 Day Plan

Makes a large pot---
2 large onions — diced
2 cans of green beans or fresh beans
2 large cans whole tomatoes or stewed
1 large head of cabbage – cubed
1 large bunch of celery – chopped
2 pkgs. onion soup mix or chicken noodle
2 lbs. of carrots – chopped
1 large can of beef or chicken broth
Season with salt, pepper, paprika, parsley. Optional – curry, cayenne, Worcestershire, bouillon

Cut vegetable into small pieces and add all ingredients to boiling water. Cook for about 10 minutes then reduce heat to simmer and continue cooking till veggies are tender.

Remember- This diet should only be followed for 7 days at a time, with at least two weeks in between.

Day One—
Fruit- Eat all of the fruit you want – except bananas. Eat only your soup and the fruit for the first day. Cantaloupe and watermelon are lower in calories than most other fruits. For drinks – unsweetened, teas, cranberry juice and water

Day Two—
Vegetables- Eat until you are stuffed with all fresh, raw or cooked vegetables of your choice. Try to eat leafy green vegetables and stay away from dry beans, peas and corn. Eat all the vegetables you want along with your soup. At dinner, reward yourself with a big baked potato with butter. Do not eat fruit today.

Day Three—
Mix days one and two- Eat all the soup, fruits and vegetables you want. NO BAKED POTATO By day three you should have lost 5 to 7 pounds if following direction.

Day Four—
Bananas and skim milk- Eat at least 3 bananas and drink as many glasses of skim milk as you would like on this day, along with your soup. Bananas are high in calories and carbohydrates as is milk but in this particular day, our body will need potassium and carbs. Proteins and calcium to lesson craving for sweets

Day Five—
Beef and Tomatoes- Ten to twenty ounces of beef and up to six fresh tomatoes. Drink at least 6 to 8 glasses of water this day to wash the uric acid from our body. Eat your soup at least once this day. You may eat broiled or baked chicken instead of beef – but absolutely no skin on chicken. If you prefer, you can substitute broiled fish for the beef on one of the beef days – but not both

Day Six—
Beef and vegetables- Eat to your heart's content of beef and vegetables this day. You can even have 2 or 3 steaks if you like, with leafy green vegetables. NO BAKED POTATO. Eat your soup at least once.

Day Seven—
Brown rice, unsweetened fruit juices and vegetables. Again stuff, stuff and stuff yourself. Be sure to eat your soup at least once this day.

By the end of 7 days, if you have not cheated on this diet, you should have lost 10 to 17 pounds, if you have lost more than 17 lbs. stay off this diet for two days before resuming this diet again.

This diet does not lend itself to drinking alcohol beverages at any time. If you must have alcohol GO OFF THIS DIET FOR AT LEAST 24 HOURS BEFORE DRINKING ANY ALCOHOL

Because everyone's digestive system is different, this diet will affect everyone differently. After 3 days, you will have more energy than when you began. After being on this diet for several days you will find that if your bowel movements have changed, eat a cup of bran or fiber.

Any prescribed medication will not hurt or affect you on this diet. Continue the diet plan as long as you wish and feel the difference both mentally and physically.

DRINK PLENTY OF WATER- AT LEAST 8 – 8 OZ GLASSES A DAY

This diet comes from the Sacred Heart Memorial Hospital and is used for overweight patients in order to lose weight rapidly, usually prior to surgery.

A Diet That Works!

This 7 day eating plan can be used as often as you like. If correctly followed, it will clean out your system of impurities and give you a feeling of well-being as never before. After only 7 days of the process, you will begin to feel lighter by a least 10 and possibly 17 lbs., and have an abundance of energy. Continue on this plan as long as you wish to feel the difference. This diet is fast, fat-burning and the secret is that you will burn more calories than you take in – this is debatable and probably not accurate. Remember everyone's body is different and results will be different.

METRIC CONVERSION CHART

VOLUME MEASUREMENT – DRY

1/8 teaspoon = 0.5 ml
¼ teaspoon = 1 ml
½ teaspoon = 2 ml
¾ teaspoon = 4 ml
1 teaspoon = 5 ml
1 tablespoon = 15 ml
2 tablespoons = 30 ml
¼ cup = 60 ml
1/3 cup = 75 ml
½ cup = 125 ml
2/3 cup = 150 ml
¾ cup = 175 ml
1 cup = 250 ml
2 cups = 1 pint = 500 ml
3 cups = 750 ml
4 cups = 1 quart = 1L

VOLUME MEASUREMENT – FLUID

1 fluid ounce = 2 tablespoons = 30 ml
4 fluid ounce = ½ cup = 125 ml
8 fluid ounce = 1 cup = 250 ml
12 fluid ounce = 1 ½ cups = 375 ml
16 fluid ounce = 2 cups = 500 ml

WEIGHTS – MASS

½ ounce = 15g
1 ounce = 30g
3 ounces = 90g
4 ounces = 129g
8 ounces = 225g
10 ounces = 285g
12 ounces = 360g
16 ounces = 1 pound = 450g

GENERAL DESCRIPTIONS

Stick of Margarine -
> Stick of margarine measures ½ cup of margarine

Powdered Sugar -
> Also known as confectioners' sugar or icing sugar, a very fine sugar.

Sugar Mix -
> A measurement of brown sugar and cinnamon mixed together.

Garlic Clove -
> One of the small bulblets that can be spilt off of the axis of a larger garlic bulb.

Baking Soda Solution -
> Baking soda dissolves in water making a transparent solution

Sour Milk -
> To make sour milk for baking, add one tablespoon of vinegar to one cup of milk or one teaspoon of lemon juice to one cup of milk.

Butter Milk -
> To make butter milk for baking, mix one cup milk with a tablespoon of vinegar or lemon juice.

Scalded Milk-
> In sauce pan, heat milk to 108 degrees F, bringing the milk to a light froth and edges will have tiny bubbles formed.

Diagonal -
> A straight line joining two opposite corners of a square, rectangle or other straight-side shape.

Lattice Top -
> Place one strip across the middle of the pie, then place two strips from the other direction across the one strip. Keep alternating the strips and you have a woven pie crust top.

GENERAL DESCRIPTIONS

Flute or Crimp Edge -
Use one hand to pinch the edge of the pie crust between your thumb and the side of your index finger.

Edging of Pie Crust -
Use a fork by holding at an angle to the edge of the pie. Lightly press the tines into the pastry. Continue around the pie, switching angles with every other press.

Hard Candy Testing -
Little syrup dropped into cold water to check on firmness and flexibility. (soft ball or hard ball)

Rice Potatoes-
A potato ricer is a kitchen tool used for pressing cooked potatoes through a bunch of holes so that the results are a uniformly smooth consistency with no lumps.

Well-
Forming a hollow in the middle of the flour dry mix.

Pat-
To take the underside of the hand and gently press a food. The purpose might be to pat dry ingredients onto the surface so they will adhere during cooking, or to pat with a towel to remove excess moisture.

Dust-
To sprinkle lightly before or after cooking with dry ingredients, such as flour, granulated or confectioners' sugar or spices.

Cheese Cloth-
A coarse, loosely woven cotton gauze, primarily in cheese making and cooking.

Pare -
To remove skins and peels from fruits or vegetables with a small knife or peeler.

Invert -
To reverse in position or to turn upside down.

Recipe for Friendship

2 heaping cups patience
1 heart full love
2 handfuls generosity
Dash of laughter
1 full cup understanding
2 cups loyalty

Mix well and sprinkle generously with kindness. Spread this irresistible delicacy over a life-time and serve everybody you meet.

Unknown Author

NOTE: When cooking with the beginner cooks in the kitchen; especially your children, remember to read this quote occasionally.

S.J. Wurst Family Farm

23862829R00155

Made in the USA
Charleston, SC
08 November 2013